HIGH TIME TO AWAKE

CRAIG C. WHITE

Jesus will fight on the Golan Heights

The nearer that Turkey gets to Israel,
the nearer that Jesus will get to Israel

CRAIG C. WHITE

Lord Jesus: Thank you for your Holy Spirit that illuminates your word in the heart of each believer and also assures us of our own salvation. Find us worthy to be spared from the trial that is coming upon the whole earth. Amen

End time Bible prophecy is happening now!

Time for Church age believers is short.

By Craig C. White

Please allow me to tell you where we are. Turkish President Erdogan is the Antichrist. No kidding. Erdogan is the "chief prince" or primary governor among the provinces of Turkey mentioned in Ezekiel chapter 38. Ezekiel says that the ruler of Turkey will lead the Islamic nations into Israel.

Ezekiel 38:1-2 And the word of the LORD came unto me, saying, 2 Son of man, set thy face against Gog, the land of Magog, the chief prince of Meshech and Tubal, and prophesy against him,

Jeremiah 49:23 mentions two northwestern Syrian cities that will hear evil reports of a coming invasion just before Damascus is destroyed. Those two cities are Hamah and Arpad. Today Arpad is called Tell-Rifaat. The Turkish Army is amassing near both of these cities right now. Turkish President Erdogan has vowed to remove Syrian President Assad from power in Damascus.

Jeremiah 49:23 Concerning Damascus. Hamath is confounded, and Arpad: for they have heard evil tidings: they are fainthearted; there is sorrow on the sea; it cannot be quiet.

The next thing that will happen is the Turkish attack on Hamah and Tell-Rifaat along with the closely following destruction of Damascus. Finally Turkey will lead the forces that are now fighting in Syria into the Golan Heights of Israel (Ezekiel 38). The Golan Heights are only thirty miles away from Damascus. I would expect to see Jesus Christ at that time!

Contents

Jesus will fight on the Golan Heights

Image credit: Whirlwind by janeblue329 (modified)
www.flickr.com

www.hightimetoawake.com

Preface

The nearer that Turkey gets to Israel, the nearer that Jesus will get to Israel

Rapture fuse is lit!

By Craig C. White

We are very near to the return of Jesus to collect his Church. It is easy to identify and to watch the events that will lead up to Jesus Christ's return. As Turkey and their allies move nearer and nearer to Israel we can know that Jesus is on his way. Jesus will return to cause the Turkish led forces to retreat when they enter the Golan Heights!

The Turkish Army has entered northern Syria. Jeremiah 49:23 lists the two northwestern cities of Hamah and Arpad. Today Arpad is called Tell Rifaat. After these cities hear "evil reports" then the residents of Damascus will flee and Damascus will be destroyed. Turkish President Erdogan said that the Turkish Army could attack these cities at any moment.

Jeremiah 49:23 Concerning Damascus. Hamath is confounded, and Arpad: for they have heard evil tidings: they are fainthearted; there is sorrow on the sea; it cannot be quiet.

After the destruction of Damascus I think that Turkey will lead the forces that are now fighting in Syria into the Golan Heights of northern Israel (Eze 38). I suspect that Jesus Christ will return to turn back the Turkish led invasion into Israel. I think that the Resurrection and Rapture will happen at that time!

In the next verse Bashan, Carmel, and Lebanon describe the Golan Heights, northern Israel, and southern Lebanon. This seems to describe Jesus as he passes above the Turkish led invaders as they enter northern Israel.

9

Nahum 1:3-7 The LORD is slow to anger, and great in power, and will not at all acquit the wicked: the LORD hath his way in the whirlwind and in the storm, and the clouds are the dust of his feet. 4 He rebuketh the sea, and maketh it dry, and drieth up all the rivers: Bashan languisheth, and Carmel, and the flower of Lebanon languisheth. 5 The mountains quake at him, and the hills melt, and the earth is burned at his presence, yea, the world, and all that dwell therein. 6 Who can stand before his indignation? and who can abide in the fierceness of his anger? his fury is poured out like fire, and the rocks are thrown down by him. 7 The LORD is good, a strong hold in the day of trouble; and he knoweth them that trust in him.

The next event to look for is the Turkish assault on Hamah. The Syrian Army is in Hamah and has announced its plans to attack nearby Idlib in September 2018. The Turkish Army is in Idlib now. Turkish President Erdogan said that Idlib is a red line for Turkey. If the Syrian Army attacks Idlib then Erdogan promises to attack the Syrian Army in Hamah.

The Rapture fuse is lit! The nearer that Turkey gets to Israel, the nearer that Jesus will get to Israel.

Chapter One

Isaiah 17 vs Jeremiah 49

The destruction of Damascus

By Craig C. White

When it comes to anticipating end time events concerning the destruction of Damascus, I wouldn't look to Isaiah chapter 17 as much as I would rely on Jeremiah 49:23-27. Isaiah 17 is primarily about the Assyrian conquest of Syria and of northern Israel in 734 BC. Isaiah 17 describes the conquest of Damascus but it also describes the fall of northern Israel. This happened in 734 BC. So Isaiah 17 has for the most part already been fulfilled. Damascus will be destroyed but I wouldn't expect to see northern Israel fall this time.

Isaiah 17:1-4   The burden of Damascus. Behold, Damascus is taken away from being a city, and it shall be a ruinous heap. 2 The cities of Aroer are forsaken: they shall be for flocks, which shall lie down, and none shall make them afraid. 3 The fortress also shall cease from Ephraim, and the kingdom from Damascus, and the remnant of Syria: they shall be as the glory of the children of Israel, saith the LORD of hosts. 4 And in that day it shall come to pass, that the glory of Jacob shall be made thin, and the fatness of his flesh shall wax lean.

Jeremiah was written one hundred years after Assyria conquered Syria. So Jeremiah is definitely about future events. Jeremiah does not describe the conquest of northern Israel. Now I think that the Turkish Army will attack northern Israel after they destroy Damascus but Turkey will not succeed in conquering northern Israel. Jesus Christ will return to fight against the Turkish led invaders when they enter the Golan Heights!

Jeremiah 49:23-27 Concerning Damascus. Hamath is confounded, and Arpad: for they have heard evil tidings: they are fainthearted; there is sorrow on the sea; it cannot be quiet. 24 Damascus is waxed feeble, and turneth herself to flee, and fear hath seized on her: anguish and sorrows have taken her, as a woman in travail. 25 How is the city of praise not left, the city of my joy! 26 Therefore her young men shall fall in her streets, and all the men of war shall be cut off in that day, saith the LORD of hosts. 27 And I will kindle a fire in the wall of Damascus, and it shall consume the palaces of Benhadad.

I know that Christians like to quote Isaiah 17:1 but that is much less relevant to end time events than is Jeremiah 49:23-27. Christians really should know better. That just goes to show you how little that Christians have actually dug into their Bibles.

Chapter Two

Russia and Iran give Turkey "safe zone" in Idlib

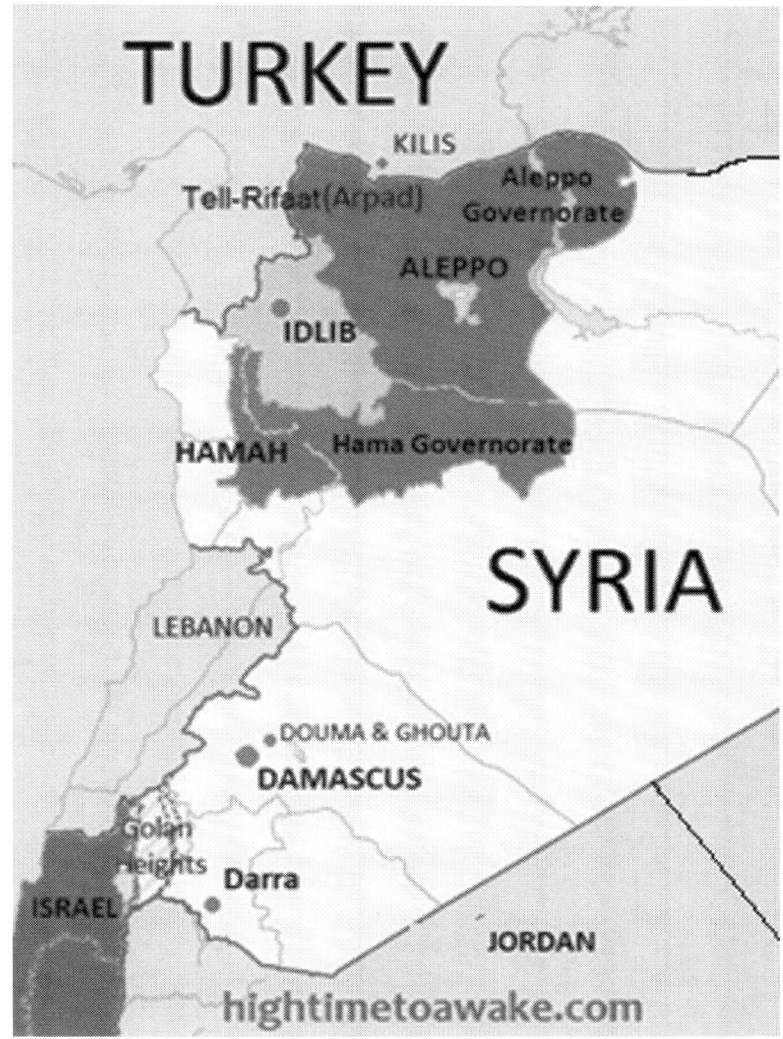

The 4 beasts of Daniel 7 exist during the end times.

By Craig C. White

Copyright 2018 Craig C. White

Turkey will soon be in position to attack Hamah

While many Christians have been looking up their Astrological charts; some real end time events have been happening on the ground.

Turkish President Erdogan has vowed to remove Syrian President Assad from power in Damascus, Syria. Iran and Russia are allied with the Syrian government. This week Iran and Russia made it a lot easier for Turkish forces to reach Damascus. Turkey has now finalized a deal with Iran and Russia to create a "safe zone" in the province of Idlib in northwestern Syria. Idlib has long been a stronghold of the Turkish supported Syrian Al-Qaeda affiliate "Ahrar al-Sham" as well as the Al-Qaeda rebel group "Hayat Tahrir al-Sham". These Al-Qaeda groups have been fighting against the Syrian Army near Hamah. Lately the Syrian Army has been winning. The "safe zone" plan will flood Idlib with an additional 25,000 Turkish troops along with Turkish supported Al-Qaeda "Free Syrian Army" rebels. What could go wrong?

The Prophet Jeremiah says that the northwestern cities of Hamah and Arpad (or modern day Tell Rifaat) will hear evil reports about a coming invasion and will be terrified. For the past few months the Turkish Army has been gathering heavy weapons and troops at Azaz, Syria in order to attack the nearby Kurdish held town of Tell Rifaat. Turkish President Erdogan said that the Turkish Army could attack Tell Rifaat at any moment. So one of the cities that Jeremiah identifies is about to be attacked by Turkish troops.

Jeremiah 49:23 Concerning Damascus. Hamath is confounded, and Arpad: for they have heard evil tidings: they are fainthearted; there is sorrow on the sea; it cannot be quiet.

With the finalized "safe zone" plan, Turkey will soon be in position to attack Hamah, the other city on Jeremiah's list. Soon Turkey will send 25,000 more Turkish and Free Syrian Army troops to Idlib located only a few miles from Hamah.

According to Jeremiah 49:23-27, after Hamah and Tell Rifaat hear evil reports of a coming invasion then the residents of Damascus will flee and Damascus will be destroyed.

Jesus said this to the religious leaders of his day.

Matthew 16:3b O ye hypocrites, ye can discern the face of the sky; but can ye not discern the signs of the times?

Christians should not be looking to the stars for a sign. Instead they should understand the events of the day. Turkey will soon be in position to attack Hamah and Tell Rifaat. This signals the soon destruction of Damascus. These are the signs of the times. It is High Time to Awake.

More from High Time to Awake

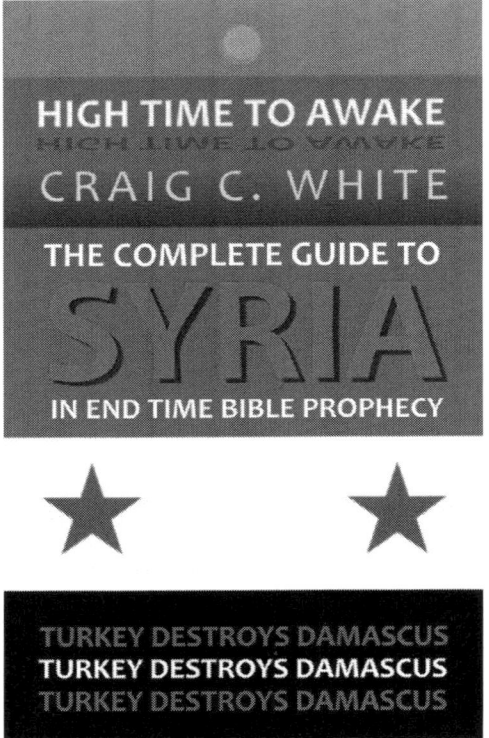

The complete guide to Syria in end time Bible Prophecy: The fuse has been burning in Syria for seven years. Now the powder keg is about to explode! Isaiah 17 predicts the destruction of Damascus, Syria.

Isa 17:1 The burden of Damascus. Behold, Damascus is taken away from being a city, and it shall be a ruinous heap.

This book contains everything that you need to know about Syria in Bible prophecy as you watch events unfold in the coming days.

Chapter Three

Turkish Army has begun its conquest of Syria!

Bible prophecy unfolding

By Craig C. White

I hope that you all have noticed! The Turkish army has been pouring into northern Syria. Turkey aims to remove the Kurdish military forces from the Afrin region of Syria. Turkey wants to eliminate the threat of an autonomous Kurdish State inside of Syria next to the Turkish border.

You might wonder why Russia hasn't objected to the Turkish attack on these Kurdish controlled towns. The U.S. supports the Kurdish troops in Syria. Turkey has convinced Russia that the Kurds now possess sophisticated U.S. arms. So Russia and Iran have now accused the U.S. of stoking the ambitions of the Kurds to create a separate Kurdish nation inside of Syria. The U.S. has countered by accusing Russia of acquiescing to the use of chemical weapons by the Syrian government.

Turkish President Erdogan told a meeting of his AK Party that Operation Euphrates Shield "drove a dagger into the heart of the game played in Syria" by the Kurds.

"We will soon also destroy one-by-one the other nests of terror in Syria, starting with Afrin and Manbij," he vowed.

"Those who stabbed us in the back and appear to be our allies... cannot prevent it," he added, apparently referring to the US.

Now for the important Bible stuff. The Prophet Jeremiah predicts the Turkish conquest of Syria. Jeremiah 49:23-27 describes the Turkish Army as they invade the northwestern Syria cities of Hamah and Arpad and then destroy Damascus. Today Arpad is called Tell Rifaat. The Turkish Army is sweeping the Afrin region from the west eastward. Tell Rifaat is on the eastern limits of the Afrin region and is

17

the key Kurdish controlled city there. The Turkish Army has stopped just outside of Tell Rifaat but Turkish President Erdogan promises to attack Tel Rifaat. In Hamah the Syrian Army is fighting and winning against the Turkish supported Al-Qaeda rebel groups in the nearby Idlib province.

Jeremiah 49:23 Concerning Damascus. Hamath is confounded, and Arpad: for they have heard evil tidings: they are fainthearted; there is sorrow on the sea; it cannot be quiet.

Jeremiah lists the city of Hamah first. So I think that we will see the Turkish Army moving towards Hamah before Jeremiah's prophecy ensues. As a matter of fact, over the past few months we have seen the Turkish Army move into Idlib in order to create a "safe zone" in northwestern Syria. The Idlib province is located right next to the Hamah province.

Jeremiah says that after Hamah and Tell Rifaat hear evil reports then the residents of Damascus will flee and Damascus will be destroyed. Afterwards I think that Turkey will then lead the forces that are now fighting in Syria into Israel. I think that Jesus will return to cause these invaders to retreat and also to gather Christians.

I have been warning people about the Turkish conquest of Syria for the past seven years. The Prophet Jeremiah has been warning us for the past 2,600 years. It is High Time for the nation of Israel and for the Christian Church to Awake.

Chapter Four

An "Extraordinary" Summit

International peace keeping force inside of Israel

By Craig C. White

It seems that biblically significant events are now happening on a daily basis. This week Israel celebrated their seventieth year anniversary of reestablishing their homeland. The U.S. dedicated their new embassy in Jerusalem. Hamas and the Palestinians protested in Gaza by attempting to break through the border fence that separates Gaza from the rest of Israel. The Israeli Defense Force shot and killed about sixty Palestinian Hamas protesters and wounded two thousand more.

It has been reported that Hamas purposefully incited the protest with the intention that people would be killed. Hamas wants to use this incident as an excuse for further military action against Israel. Enter Turkish President Erdogan.

Responding to the Gaza killings Turkish President Erdogan said that, "Turkey will not allow Israel to steal Jerusalem from Palestinians". Erdogan called for all Islamic nations to unite against Israel and vowed to take Jerusalem for Islam.

This week Turkish President Erdogan called for an "extraordinary" summit of the 57 Islamic nation members "Organization for Islamic Cooperation" (OIC). The OIC is the largest voting bloc in the UN. Erdogan is currently the head of the OIC. At the May 18th meeting Erdogan condemned Israel's actions during the Gaza incident and also condemned the inauguration of the American embassy. Erdogan proposed that an international peace keeping force be placed inside of Israel.

Folks this is sounding more and more like the seven year covenant that the Antichrist will make with Israel. The Antichrist will promise peace with Israel in exchange for a new temple in Jerusalem and disarmament of Israel along with an international peace keeping force being placed inside of Israel.

Now do you believe me when I say that Turkish President Erdogan is the Antichrist?

Chapter Five

If Erdogan wins election he will become the most powerful ruler of Turkey since Ataturk!

Turkey election Sun June 24th 2018

By Craig C. White

Turkey has a huge Presidential election on June 24th. If Turkish President Erdogan wins the election he will become the official dictator of Turkey with sweeping new powers. Erdogan said that he called for the early election because he wants to push further into Syria. Turkey is already reclaiming some northwestern Syrian provinces as part of a revived Ottoman Empire.

I don't get many sensible replies to my Bible analysis. Lately people have been arguing that Erdogan will lose the election and never be heard from again. Don't be naive my friends. Just like the Bible says; Turkish President Erdogan will succeed in magnifying himself. Even if somehow Erdogan manages to loose Sunday's election, when the dust settles he will emerge as the Sultan over all of Islam.

Daniel 8:25 And through his policy also he shall cause craft to prosper in his hand; and he shall magnify himself in his heart, and by peace shall destroy many:

This is no ordinary election. Erdogan personally fashioned this election to give himself great power. Last year Erdogan conducted a national referendum in Turkey to change the Turkish constitution. Up until now the office of president has only been ceremonial but after Sunday's election the new president will be given almost complete control over the legal system, government, military, and national police. Two months ago Erdogan himself set this election's rushed date. Don't forget that Erdogan spent the past two years confiscating nearly all independent news and media outlets in Turkey to use as his own propaganda machines. That means that Erdogan either forcibly took or purchased nearly every national newspaper and television network in Turkey. Nearly all of the campaign coverage has been promoting Erdogan. Do you really think that Erdogan will allow himself to lose this election?

Not to mention this! I know that western Christians are nearly completely out of touch BUT Muslims around the world are looking to Turkish President Erdogan to be named as *Sultan* and to reestablish the Ottoman Empire. This didn't happen overnight folks. The Muslim world has been looking to Erdogan to unite all of Islam under a new Caliphate for the past dozen years. After Turkey's failed coup in 2016, top Muslim clerics from nearly every Islamic nation formally pledged their written allegiance to Erdogan as their promised Mahdi.

My friends, we do not need to wonder who the Antichrist is; or if Turkish President will succeed or not. I have been telling people that Turkish President Erdogan is the Antichrist from the scripture for seven years. He is the "chief prince" or primary governor among the provinces of Turkey as described in Ezekiel 38:1-3. The term "chief prince" is a perfect way of saying "prime minister". Thanks to Erdogan there will be no future Prime Minister of Turkey. Erdogan has changed the Turkish constitution and eliminated the position of Prime Minister. Erdogan was Prime Minister for twelve years. He is the only person in history who can be identified as the chief prince of Turkey who has clawed his way up to the top position of power in Turkey.

Erdogan has already done several things that identify him as being the Antichrist. He has built the largest mosque dedicated to himself as the Sultan of the Ottoman Empire in Istanbul. He built the tents of his tabernacle between the seas on the Bosporus. The Islamic world has been eagerly anticipating the rise of Sultan Erdogan. As a matter of fact Erdogan's campaign slogan is "It's Time". That means that "It's Time" to establish the true Islamic Caliphate!

Erdogan has vowed to conquer Damascus and also Egypt. Turkish President Erdogan has rallied the Islamic nations against the Golan Heights and also against Jerusalem. What more do you want from the Antichrist? Turkish President Erdogan is the Antichrist. There is no need to look for another.

And another thing! Consider the timing of this election. Right now the Turkish Army is amassed near Hamah and Tell Rifaat in northwestern Syria. Tell Rifaat is called Arpad in Jeremiah 49:23 below. Erdogan called for this early election because he wants to attack these areas. The Bible tells us that he will succeed.

Jeremiah 49:23 Concerning Damascus. Hamath is confounded, and Arpad: for they have heard evil tidings: they are fainthearted; there is sorrow on the sea; it cannot be quiet.

Jeremiah says that after Hamah and Tell Rifaat hear evil reports then Damascus will be destroyed. Also, every nation that is listed in Ezekiel 38:5 is now fighting in Syria. After Turkey destroys Damascus then Turkey will lead the Iranian Army, Hezbollah, the Free Syrian Army (Al-Qaeda from Libya and Sudan), and every other Al-Qaeda faction and other rebel groups into the Golan Heights of northern Israel.

Do you prefer waking up to soothing music or do you prefer air-raid sirens? Don't hit the snooze button. Turkish President Erdogan is the Antichrist. It is High Time to Awake!

More from High Time to Awake

Available from Amazon.com, CreateSpace.com, and other retail outlets. Also available on Kindle and other devices.

Our Salvation is Nearer! is filled with reports about the prophetic world events that signify the last days of the Church age. These events are happening now. The day of the Resurrection and Rapture of Church age believers in Jesus Christ is rapidly approaching. The countdown to the Rapture shouldn't be measured in years and years, but the day of resurrection and the gathering together to meet Jesus Christ in the air should now be expected in months to perhaps a couple of years.

hightimetoawake.com

Chapter Six

It's easy to see who the Antichrist is

Because the Bible tells us what he will do

By Craig C. White

Turkish President Erdogan is the Antichrist. It is easy to see. The Antichrist will reestablish the Turkish ruled Ottoman Empire. Top Muslim clerics from almost every Islamic nation have already pledged their allegiance to Erdogan as their promised Mahdi. Erdogan has built the largest Mosque in Turkey for himself on the Bosporus between the seas in Istanbul (Dan 11:45). Erdogan is the "Assyrian" which is a type of the Antichrist. The Antichrist isn't from Assyria (or northern Iraq today). But the Antichrist will do the same things that the Assyrian kings did. He will conquer Syria (and destroy Damascus; Jeremiah 49:23). He will then invade northern Israel (Ezekiel 38).

Jeremiah 49:23 Concerning Damascus. Hamath is confounded, and Arpad: for they have heard evil tidings: they are fainthearted; there is sorrow on the sea; it cannot be quiet.

Turkish President Erdogan has promised to remove Syrian President Assad from power in Damascus. Jeremiah tells us that the destruction of Damascus will begin at Hamah and Arpad in northwestern Syria. The Turkish Army is already amassed near Hamah and Tell-Rifaat (Tell Rifaat is called Arpad in Jer 49:23). Erdogan said that the Turkish Army could attack Tell-Rifaat at any moment. The Turkish Army is also now in Idlib, Syria. Idlib is located just to the north of Hamah. The Turkish Army is about to attack Hamah and Tell-Rifaat (Arpad) just like the Prophet Jeremiah said. Then the Turkish Army along with its Al-Qaeda allies will march southward to destroy Damascus.

Turkish President Erdogan has also called on the Islamic nations to take back the Golan Heights. After Turkey destroys Damascus they will lead the forces that are now fighting in Syria into northern Israel. Every nation that Ezekiel 38:5 lists is now fighting in Syria; namely Iran (Iranian Guard and Hezbollah), Sudan and Libya (Free Syrian Army).

Ezekiel 38:5 Persia, Ethiopia, and Libya with them; all of them with shield and helmet:

It is no secret that Turkish President Erdogan intends to reestablish the Ottoman Empire with himself as its ruler. According to Revelation 13:3 the seventh world empire (or the Turkish ruled Ottoman Empire) will be healed. The first nation on Erdogan's hit list is Syria with Egypt following closely behind. Once Turkey conquers Syria, Erdogan says that he will install a Muslim Brotherhood leader there. Then Turkey, Syria, Iraq, and Iran will form a Union (Rev 9:14) with other Islamic nations following like Libya and Sudan.

Daniel 11:42 tells us that the Antichrist will conquer northern Africa and that Egypt will not escape.

Dan 11:42 He shall stretch forth his hand also upon the countries: and the land of Egypt shall not escape. 43 But he shall have power over the treasures of gold and of silver, and over all the precious things of Egypt: and the Libyans and the Ethiopians *shall be* at his steps.

Turkish President Erdogan has promised to reinstate ousted Muslim Brotherhood President Mohamed Morsi back into power in Egypt. Turkey is building a large naval personnel carrier for that purpose. Daniel 11:42 says that Libya and Sudan will be in league with the Antichrist as he invades northern Africa. Libya and Sudan are already fighting alongside Turkey in Syria today. The Bible tells us that all of these things are the actions of the Antichrist. Turkish President Erdogan has told the world that he will do all of these things. Turkish President Erdogan is the Antichrist. It is easy to see.

The next thing that will happen is the attack on Hamah and Tell-Rifaat along with the closely following destruction of Damascus. Then Turkey will lead the forces that are now fighting in Syria into the Golan Heights of Israel only thirty miles away from Damascus. I would expect to see Jesus Christ at that time!

Available from Amazon.com, CreateSpace.com, and other retail outlets. Also available on Kindle and other devices.

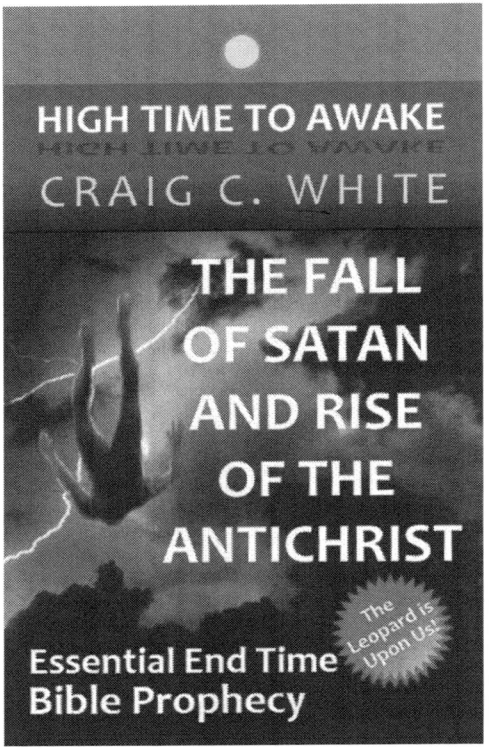

The Fall of Satan and Rise of the Antichrist explains how the Antichrist is the sign of the Rapture. This book contains "The Leopard is Upon Us!" about the formation of the final gentile world empire. It also looks at Mystery Babylon from a fly's eye view.

www.hightimetoawake.com

Chapter Seven

When will the Antichrist sit in the temple?

During the middle of the Tribulation period

By Craig C. White

Turkish President Erdogan is the Antichrist but when will he sit in the Temple? Well first there has to be a new temple built in Jerusalem, right? I think that permission to build a new Jewish temple will be a part of the seven year term treaty that the Antichrist will make concerning Israel (Daniel 9:27). I think that Erdogan will sit in the new temple in Jerusalem when Turkey attacks Judea and Jerusalem during the middle of the seven year long Tribulation period. This will begin Jerusalem's *great tribulation*.

In 2Thessalonians the Apostle Paul lists two events that must proceed the Tribulation period. They are the fall of Satan from heaven to earth, and the revealing of the Antichrist.

2Thessalonians 2:2-3 That ye be not soon shaken in mind, or be troubled, neither by spirit, nor by word, nor by letter as from us, as that the day of Christ is at hand. 3 Let no man deceive you by any means: for that day shall not come, except there come a falling away first, and that man of sin be revealed, the son of perdition;

In the next verse Paul talks about the Antichrist as he sits in the temple of God showing himself that he is God.

2Thessalonians 2:4 Who opposeth and exalteth himself above all that is called God, or that is worshipped; so that he as God sitteth in the temple of God, shewing himself that he is God.

I think that the Antichrist will sit in the temple a few years after the fall of Satan and the revealing of the Antichrist with signs and lying wonders.

2Thessalonians 2:9 Even him, whose coming is after the working of Satan with all power and signs and lying wonders,

I think that Jesus will return for his Church long before this happens. Turkey will invade Jerusalem and Judea during the middle of the seven year Tribulation period. Jesus warns the residents of Judea to WATCH and to flee as the armies of the Antichrist approaches.

Matthew 24:42 Watch therefore: for ye know not what hour your Lord doth come.

Matthew 24:42 is part of a parable. The word "Lord" here does not refer to Jesus Christ. The parable is a warning to watch for somebody coming unexpectedly. The Antichrist will make a surprise ambush on Jerusalem.

Matthew 24:15 When ye therefore shall see the abomination of desolation, spoken of by Daniel the prophet, stand in the holy place, (whoso readeth, let him understand:)

This day will begin Jerusalem's great tribulation. This is the day that no man knows the time that the Antichrist's armies will attack Jerusalem.

Matthew 24:36 But of that day and hour knoweth no man, no, not the angels of heaven, but my Father only.

I know that most people say that this verse is talking about the Rapture of the Church but they are WRONG! Matthew chapter 24 is written to the Jews living around Jerusalem during the tribulation period. Jesus is warning them about the invasion of Jerusalem. Matthew chapter 24 has nothing at all to do with the Church.

Chapter Eight

He shall plant the tabernacles of his palace between the seas in the glorious holy mountain

Turkish President Erdogan has built his mosque between the seas on the Bosporus on Istanbul's highest hill

By Craig C. White

Besides building the largest palace in the world in Turkey's capital city of Ankara; Turkish President Erdogan is on a building spree of Mosques in Istanbul.

Daniel 11:45 And he shall plant the tabernacles of his palace between the seas in the glorious holy mountain; yet he shall come to his end, and none shall help him.

Daniel 11:45 says that the Antichrist will "plant the tabernacles of his palace between the seas in the glorious holy mountain". Turkish President Erdogan is building several Mosques in Istanbul including a controversial Mosque in Taksim square. Taksim square has long been a site dedicated to Mustafa Kemal Atatürk founder of the republic of Turkey and proponent of Turkey's western philosophy. By building a Mosque in Taksim square Erdogan is shunning Turkey's one hundred years of democracy and is moving Turkey back towards its Ottoman Empire Islamist ways.

Erdogan has also built the largest Mosque in Turkey. The Çamlıca Mosque overlooks the Bosporus connecting the Black Sea to the Sea of Marmara, Aegean Sea, and Mediterranean Sea. Every Mosque in Istanbul could be described as being between the seas. But the Çamlıca Mosque is built right on the Bosporus at the highest elevation in Istanbul. The Çamlıca Mosque was inaugurated on July 1, 2016. The Çamlıca Mosque is dedicated to the Sultan of the Ottoman Empire. So Erdogan evidently anticipates the revival of the Ottoman Empire. Every past Sultan of the Ottoman Empire has built a Mosque dedicated

31

to himself. Obviously Erdogan is identifying himself as the new Turkish Sultan and rightful ruler of all of Islam.

Chapter Nine

What is the abomination of desolation?

By Craig C. White

The Prophet Daniel describes an action that will bring desolation upon Jerusalem and pollute its new temple. It is called the abomination of desolation.

Daniel 9:27 And he shall confirm the covenant with many for one week: and in the midst of the week he shall cause the sacrifice and the oblation to cease, and for the overspreading of abominations he shall make it desolate, even until the consummation, and that determined shall be poured upon the desolate.

The abomination that makes desolate is an action that desecrates the next temple to be built in Jerusalem. During the middle of the seven year long Tribulation period the Antichrist will either; sit in the temple and proclaim that he should be worshiped as god; or he will erect an image or idol in the temple that claims that he is god.

2Thessalonians 2:4 Who opposeth and exalteth himself above all that is called God, or that is worshipped; so that he as God sitteth in the temple of God, shewing himself that he is God.

Matthew 24:15-17 When ye therefore shall see the abomination of desolation, spoken of by Daniel the prophet, stand in the holy place, (whoso readeth, let him understand:) 16 Then let them which be in Judaea flee into the mountains: 17 Let him which is on the housetop not come down to take any thing out of his house:

The action of desecrating the temple will usher in a three and one half year period of God's indignation towards Israel. During this time the enemies of Israel will overrun Jerusalem. God has determined three and one half years of suffering for Jerusalem. At the end of this time the nation of

33

Israel will remember that their God is faithful to keep his promise to never leave or forsake his people Israel. Jesus Christ will return to rescue the last remaining Jews in Jerusalem and vanquish Israel's enemies.

Chapter Ten

Will the mark of the beast be worldwide?

Microchips are best served with a grain of salt.

By Craig C. White

Revelation 13:16 says that during the Tribulation all people must receive a mark on their right hand or on their foreheads in order to buy or sell. This is called "the mark of the beast". This beast represents the next world empire. So the mark of the beast identifies you as a faithful follower of the next world empire. This leads me to ask, "Will the next world empire really cover the entire world?" "Does the word "all" really mean all people in the entire world?" The Bible sheds light on these questions.

Revelation 13:16 And he causeth all, both small and great, rich and poor, free and bond, to receive a mark in their right hand, or in their foreheads: 17 And that no man might buy or sell, save he that had the mark, or the name of the beast, or the number of his name. 18 Here is wisdom. Let him that hath understanding count the number of the beast: for it is the number of a man; and his number is Six hundred threescore and six.

A fanciful idea has sprung up and has also taken root in Christian circles; the idea that every person in the entire world will be faced with the decision of receiving a microchip identification implant in their right hand or in their forehead. If you accept this microchip then you are going to hell! This keeps Christians up at night. They are awaiting the announcement, "The world is instituting a mandatory microchip ID program!" The Bible does say that a mark will be worn. But it doesn't specifically define a microchip. The Bible doesn't specifically say that all of the world will be subject to the mark of the next world empire. I can prove it.

Bible scholars say that one of the ancient world empires will be revived during the Tribulation period. Many identify this world empire as being a revived Roman Empire (which is a mistake). Others identify this end time empire as being a revived Turkish ruled Ottoman Empire (which is correct). Either way, everybody agrees that a previous world empire will be reestablished. Now we must ask ourselves, "Did any past world empire cover the entire geographic area of the world?" The answer is absolutely not. So the next world empire cannot cover the entire geographic area of the world. Otherwise it would not be an old world empire that has been revived but it would have to be categorized as some new kind of world empire altogether. Like every past world empire I would expect that the next world empire will cover roughly the geographic area between Europe and India including northern Africa. This by and large identifies the Islamic world today. You should recognize that these are also the only nations that the Bible calls by name.

Then who will be asked to wear the mark of the next world empire? Well it follows that the people who live in the region of the next world empire will be required to wear the identifying mark of the next world empire. Today all Muslims living in the region of the former Turkish ruled Ottoman Empire already wear the identifying mark of Islam. They all wear the "bismillah" on their right arms or on their foreheads. The bismillah is an armband or headband with the Arabic words saying "In the name of Allah" written on them. The bismillah is worn by every Islamic sect from Morocco to India. Now allow me to tell you something even more astonishing. The three Greek letters that spell "six hundred sixty six" are the same Arabic characters that spell "In the name of Allah". It seems that the mark of Islam will be the mark of the next world empire. There are no microchips needed.

When Bible prophecy is written about world events it is typically about how these events affect Israel. So I would expect that the mark of the next world empire will also be applied in Israel. This would certainly cause hardship for Israeli Jews who honor the God of their fathers; Abraham,

Isaac, and Jacob. Although let me point out that during talks with Turkish religious leaders regarding building a new Jewish Temple in Jerusalem, several top Israeli rabbis have already agreed that Israel and Islam serve the same God. It is conceivable that these rabbis would even be willing to wear the Islamic armband for the sake of peace; the chief among these rabbis being temple activist and Israeli Parliament member Rabbi Yehuda Glick.

Turkish President Erdogan intends to unite the Islamic world under Turkish rule. Erdogan intends to recreate the Turkish ruled Ottoman Empire. Islam promises an empire that will rule the world. Many Islamic nations are already on-board with Erdogan as their promised Mahdi. Syria isn't. That is why Turkey will conquer Syria and destroy Damascus. But I digress.

The Micro-chipping of every world citizen has become an indisputable doctrine in the Christian Church. But that is mere fantasy. The mark of the beast identifies you as a faithful follower of the next world empire. The next world empire will not include the entire world. The next world empire will cover the same geographic area of a past world empire. When it comes to microchips they are best served with a grain of salt. Oh and with guacamole of course!

More from High Time to Awake

Available from Amazon.com, CreateSpace.com, and other retail outlets. Also available on Kindle and other devices.

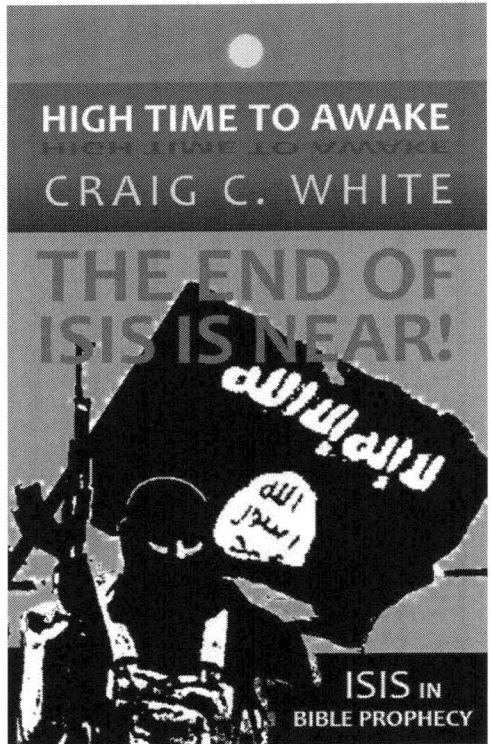

The End of ISIS is near thoroughly covers ISIS in Bible prophecy. It also contains a collection of commentaries about present day prophecy whose subjects are current and widely varied.

What is really going on in the world? Will Al-Qaeda take Baghdad? Is all the fighting in the Middle East related? Why is Russia creating a Union? Has Egypt seen the last of the Muslim Brotherhood? What is the Pope up to? Will the Turkey-Israeli reconciliation agreement have a seven year term?

hightimetoawake.com

Chapter Eleven

Will the Antichrist be received as a great peace maker or as a Jewish Messiah?

Not necessarily so.

By Craig C. White

Daniel 11:21 says that the Antichrist will "come in peaceably". Many Christians think that this means that the Antichrist will be received as a great peace maker or even be accepted as a Jewish Messiah. The Bible doesn't tell us that the Antichrist will be received as a Jewish Messiah; although he is already being received as an Islamic Mahdi.

Daniel describes a leader who will come in "come in peaceably". This saying is first applied to Antiochous Epiphanies. Antiochous Epiphanies was a prince in the Seleucid dynasty. The Seleucid dynasty ruled over one quarter of the Grecian Empire and has headquartered in Antioch of Syria. Antiochous Epiphanies' brother was the king over the Seleucid dynasty. Then one day Antiochous Epiphanies' brother was imprisoned in Egypt. While the king was in prison, the king's infant son was made king. Antiochous Epiphanies proclaimed himself as co-regent with the young boy and then killed his brother's son making himself sole ruler over the Seleucid dynasty. So Antiochous Epiphanies became king by treacherous means. That's what the word "flatteries" means at the end of Dan 11:21. Antiochous Epiphanies became king without military conquest. He gained power "peaceably".

Dan 11:21 And in his estate shall stand up a vile person, to whom they shall not give the honour of the kingdom: but he shall come in peaceably, and obtain the kingdom by flatteries.

Now that you have had your Bible history lesson, let's see what Daniel says about future events. Most Bible teachers also apply Daniel 11:21 to the actions of the coming Antichrist.

Turkish President Erdogan has just gained absolute authority over Turkey. He did so by changing the Turkish constitution and eliminating the position of Prime Minister in Turkey. Ezekiel 38:1-3 says that the "chief prince" or primary governor of Turkey will lead the Islamic nations into Israel. In Ezekiel chapter 39 the "chief prince" of Turkey will lead the battle of Armageddon. So the Bible tells us that the "chief prince" of Turkey is the Antichrist. Since Turkish President Erdogan has eliminated any future Prime Minister in Turkey, then Erdogan will be the only primary governor of Turkey in the foreseeable future. I think that Turkish President Erdogan is in fact the Antichrist. He has already come to power by way of treachery and without military conquest, or "peaceably". Erdogan will one day also rise to power over the next world empire. Erdogan is already recognized by most Islamic nations as the rightful Sultan over a revived Turkish ruled Ottoman Empire.

Many Christians have a fuzzy notion that the Antichrist will be viewed as a great peace maker. Not necessarily so. In reality the Antichrist will gain power by devious political means.

Chapter Twelve

Kidnap Gulen?

Head of the last world empire would be healed

By Craig C. White

Reports have surfaced about an alleged plot to bring Turkish Cleric Fethullah Gulen back to Turkey.

Turkish Muslim Cleric Fethullah Gulen has millions of followers around the world but especially in Turkey. Fethullah Gulen has told his followers that one day he will return to Turkey as the chief Imam of a revived Ottoman Empire. Turkish President Erdogan chased Gulen out of Turkey because Gulen ran a vast underground organization that threatened Erdogan's power. Gulen fled Turkey and is living in a palatial estate in Pennsylvania under CIA protection. Turkish President Erdogan has been demanding that Gulen be returned to Turkey.

If Fethullah Gulen returns to Turkey and recognizes Erdogan as the rightful Sultan of a revived Turkish ruled Ottoman Empire then the head of the last world empire would be healed. Together Erdogan and Gulen would have the support of nearly every Turkish citizen as well as the support of nearly every Islamic nation.

Revelation 13:3 And I saw one of his heads as it were wounded to death; and his deadly wound was healed: and all the world wondered after the beast.

Turkish President Erdogan has made it no secret that he intends to become the Sultan over a revived Turkish ruled Ottoman Empire. He already has the support of many Islamic nations and rulers. The first nation to fall under Turkish conquest will be Syria. The Prophet Jeremiah describes the Turkish Army as they march through northwestern Syria past Hamah and Tell Rifaat (Arpad) and then march southward to destroy Damascus. After the

41

destruction of Damascus, Turkey will lead the forces that are fighting in Syria today into the Golan Heights of Israel (Eze 38). Turkish President Erdogan is the Antichrist. If he reconciles with Gulen then he would gain his False Prophet and would become the undisputed king over the entire Muslim world. Erdogan would be recognized as the promised Islamic Mahdi, Sultan, Caliph, and Antichrist.

Chapter Thirteen

Jewish and Christian conservatives promote building new temple in Jerusalem

This will usher in Jerusalem's great tribulation.

By Craig C. White

The latest troubling news that I have heard is that conservative Christian Bible teachers and conservative Jewish pundits are all calling for a temple to be built in Jerusalem. They say that this will usher in lasting peace in Israel. But in truth, building a temple in Jerusalem will usher in Jerusalem's great tribulation. Some people who have promoted building a new temple in Jerusalem are Rabbi Yehudah Glick of course but also former Arkansas Governor and Evangelical Christian Mike Huckabee, Jewish conservative activist and lawyer Jay Sekulow, almost every born again Jewish believer, and some conservative Bible teachers.

Mike Huckabee has joined forces with Rabbi Yehudah Glick for the purpose of gathering signatures on the Jerusalem Covenant. The Jerusalem Covenant is a petition that reaffirms Israel's right to exist as a nation and also it's right to build a temple in Jerusalem. Rabbi Yehudah Glick is an Israeli Parliament (Knesset) member plus Glick is also the leading proponent for building a temple in Jerusalem.

Conservative Radio and TV talk show host and lawyer Jay Sekulow recently gave a speech at the UN calling for Israel's right to build a temple in Jerusalem. I love Jay Sekulow. He truly does fight for law and justice; but he should be aware that the Prophet Daniel says that building a temple in Jerusalem and resuming temple sacrifices there will hasten the time of Jacob's trouble.

A few conservative Christian Bible teachers seem to think that the Ezekiel chapter 38 invasion into Israel will usher in lasting peace. The Turkish led Ezekiel chapter 38 invasion into Israel is forming now in Syria. Every nation that Ezekiel 38:5 lists is fighting in Syria today.

Ezekiel 38:5 Persia, Ethiopia, and Libya with them; all of them with shield and helmet:

It's true that God will cause these nations to retreat. But the Turkish led Ezekiel chapter 38 invasion into Israel will likely prompt the seven year peace treaty spoken of by the Prophet Daniel. This seven year treaty will be broken in the middle of its term by an attack on Jerusalem; thus beginning Jerusalem's three and one half years of great tribulation.

Daniel 9:27 And he shall confirm the covenant with many for one week: and in the midst of the week he shall cause the sacrifice and the oblation to cease, and for the overspreading of abominations he shall make it desolate, even until the consummation, and that determined shall be poured upon the desolate.

It just proves that it is not enough to be conservative. You must be born again and filled with the Holy Spirit. You also must understand scripture. There is a way that seems right to a man but the end thereof is destruction.

The next verse was written about the Jews living around Jerusalem. When they declare that peace and security has finally come to Jerusalem then an army will sweep in and kill them or carry them away as prisoners.

1Thessalonians 5:3 For when they shall say, Peace and safety; then sudden destruction cometh upon them, as travail upon a woman with child; and they shall not escape.

Today the Jewish Rabbis are predicting that building a temple will bring lasting peace to Jerusalem. Jewish and Christian conservatives are reinforcing this treacherous misconception. The Tribulation truly is near. It's High Time to Awake!

44

Chapter Fourteen

Christians are being LEFT BEHIND!!!

I wonder if they will be left behind

By Craig C. White

Are you being left behind? Most Christians today are. When I say "left behind" you probably think about being left behind on earth after Jesus Christ returns for his Church. I hate to break the news but being left behind is a possibility. But I am talking about being left behind in your understanding of end time events that are happening right now. We can see several end time events that the Bible has predicted happening right now and that are just about to happen. It is actually pretty easy to spot these events if you understand Bible prophecy, and if you know a little bit about world history, plus a little geography. I am guessing that most Christians today haven't got a grasp on any of these subjects. I am here to tell you that time is running out for you to start learning. Sorry for the harsh words but it's my job to afflict the comfortable.

2Timothy 4:2 Preach the word; be instant in season, out of season; reprove, rebuke, exhort with all longsuffering and doctrine.

Guess what? Turkey is about to attack Hamah and Tell Rifaat in northwestern Syria just like Jeremiah 49:23 predicts. After that Turkey will destroy Damascus (Isaiah 17:1, Jeremiah 49:23-27) and then lead the forces that are fighting in Syria today into the Golan Heights of Israel (Eze 38). Very few people can see these events coming, but they are as plain as can be. Most Christians are stuck looking at the stars but you can stop looking up and begin looking around you. Turkish President Erdogan is the Antichrist. Turkey is the end time invader of Israel mentioned in Ezekiel chapter 38. Before Turkey invades Israel they will destroy Damascus. While talking about Syria, Turkish President

Erdogan has said repeatedly that the Turkish Army *could come one night unexpectedly and all at once.*

Did you know that ISIS leader Al-Baghdadi recently recorded a message to his troops? Did you know that his message is mentioned in Nahum 2:5? Will you know that when Jesus asks you about it? The northern Iraq city of Mosul is the hometown of Al-Baghdadi and of ISIS. Modern day Mosul is built around the ruins of the ancient Assyrian capital city of Nineveh. Nineveh is mentioned in the Bible. A lot of Bible prophecy that was written about Nineveh has already been fulfilled in Mosul. Some very dramatic events are still yet to come.

Are you keeping up or are you falling behind? I am seeing Christians drifting further and further away from a true understanding of end time biblical predictions. I wonder how far away they will be by the time that Jesus Christ returns? Will they allow themselves to fall so far behind that Jesus will actually leave them behind? You don't think that that could happen?

Here are the warnings that Jesus gave to the seven Churches in Revelation. He is saying that when he comes, Christians had better be alert or there will be consequences. It seems to me that he is implying that lukewarm Christians will be forced to endure the Tribulation on earth.

Rev 2:5 Remember therefore from whence thou art fallen, and repent, and do the first works; or else I will come unto thee quickly, and will remove thy candlestick out of his place, except thou repent.

Rev 2:16 Repent; or else I will come unto thee quickly, and will fight against them with the sword of my mouth.

Rev 3:3 Remember therefore how thou hast received and heard, and hold fast, and repent. If therefore thou shalt not watch, I will come on thee as a thief, and thou shalt not know what hour I will come upon thee.

Rev 3:11 Behold, I come quickly: hold that fast which thou hast, that no man take thy crown.

Rev 3:16 So then because thou art lukewarm, and neither cold nor hot, I will spue thee out of my mouth.

The letters to the seven Churches in Revelation are meant for every Church age believer. They mean something. As far as Christians being left behind goes, Jesus tells us to be ready or there will be bad consequences. Trouble comes to Jerusalem like a thief in the night. That means that Jerusalem will suffer great tribulation suddenly and unexpectedly. That is what Jesus promises for unprepared Christians in Rev 3:3.

More from High Time to Awake

Available from Amazon.com, CreateSpace.com, and other retail outlets. Also available on Kindle and other devices.

Welcome to the end times. You're late! Just to be certain that we are all aware; the Antichrist is now identifiable. The one sign that Jesus will give to Israel that proves he is truly their God is set to happen any day. Big trouble is about to come on earth. Jesus Christ is about to come with a trumpet call to raise the dead and to take away Christians. Jesus is coming. Not in five years but very very soon!

Welcome to the end times lists the biblical end times events that we can already see happening today!

www.hightimetoawake.com

Chapter Fifteen

Church age Christians should not look for signs in the heavens

Heavenly signs are meant for Israel near the end of their great tribulation

By Craig C. White

The only signs in the heavens happen near the end of the Tribulation period. These signs are meant for the Jews who are being horribly persecuted in Jerusalem and Judea. These signs are meant to comfort Israel; showing them that Jesus Christ their Messiah is coming to rescue them soon. There are no heavenly signs that Church age Christians should look for except maybe Satan as he falls from heaven to earth like a brightly shining star.

Luke 21:25-27 And there shall be signs in the sun, and in the moon, and in the stars; and upon the earth distress of nations, with perplexity; the sea and the waves roaring; 26 Men's hearts failing them for fear, and for looking after those things which are coming on the earth: for the powers of heaven shall be shaken. 27 And then shall they see the Son of man coming in a cloud with power and great glory.

In Joel 2:31 we are told that there will be signs in the sun and the moon before Jesus Christ's second coming.

Joel 2:30-32 And I will shew wonders in the heavens and in the earth, blood, and fire, and pillars of smoke. 31 The sun shall be turned into darkness, and the moon into blood, before the great and the terrible day of the LORD come. 32 And it shall come to pass, that whosoever shall call on the name of the LORD shall be delivered: for in mount Zion and in Jerusalem shall be deliverance, as the LORD hath said, and in the remnant whom the LORD shall call.

Notice that these verses directly relate to the nation of Israel. The sun will be darkened and the moon will become blood red. These signs will indicate the approaching judgment of God on Israel's enemies. These signs will likely be most visible in Jerusalem. Verse 32 above indicates that Jews will be rescued on Mt. Zion. Mt. Zion is the hill just south of the temple mount in Jerusalem. There will be a small group of Jews on Mount Zion who will survive the Tribulation (please read my commentary titled "The Last Jews in Jerusalem"). Below, Revelation 6:12 is quoting Joel 2:31.

Rev 6:12 And I beheld when he had opened the sixth seal, and, lo, there was a great earthquake; and the sun became black as sackcloth of hair, and the moon became as blood;

It is important to note that according to these verses these signs do not foretell the approach of the Resurrection or Rapture. Nor do they foretell the coming of the Tribulation period. Instead these verses most certainly pertain to the end of the seven year Tribulation period. They foretell the day of Jesus Christ's vengeance and wrath on Israel's enemies. Before Jesus returns in power and vengeance against Israel's enemies the sun shall be turned into darkness, and the moon into blood. These signs will be visible to the Jews bunkered on Mount Zion. Before Jesus returns to vanquish Israel's enemies and to save the surviving Jews in Jerusalem there will be signs in the heavens and in the earth.

In the verse below, Jesus confirms that these signs occur near the end of the Tribulation period.

Matthew 24:29 Immediately after the tribulation of those days shall the sun be darkened, and the moon shall not give her light, and the stars shall fall from heaven, and the powers of the heavens shall be shaken:

Jesus said this to the religious leaders of his day.

Matthew 16:3b O ye hypocrites, ye can discern the face of the sky; but can ye not discern the signs of the times?

Christians should not be looking to the stars for a sign. Instead they should understand the events of the day. Turkey will soon be in position to attack Hamah and Tell Rifaat. This signals that the destruction of Damascus is near. ISIS leader Abu Bakr Al-Baghdadi just recorded a message to his ISIS troops just like Nahum 2:5 predicted. This tells us that the city of Mosul in northern Iraq is about to be flooded and may indicate the near coming of Jesus Christ. These are the signs of the times. Don't be left in the dark. It's High Time to understand end time Bible prophecy. It's High Time to understand the signs of the times.

Chapter Sixteen

We should expect to see a bright shining light in the heavens as Satan hurtles though space towards earth!

Copyright 2012, 2012 Craig C. White

By Craig C. White

Considering the fact that world events suggest a near time destruction of Damascus and a subsequent Turkish led invasion into Israel, this has been on my mind more of late. Before Turkey leads the forces that are now fighting in Syria into northern Israel, we should expect to see a bright shining light in the heavens as Satan hurtles though space towards earth!

I know that everybody thinks that "a falling away" in **2Thessalonians 2:3** is the apostasy of the Church but everybody is WRONG! A falling away is the casting out of Satan from heaven to earth. Satan must fall from heaven before he can empower the Antichrist. These two things must happen before the Tribulation begins. So Christians really should not be surprised when they see Satan falling through outer space like lightning. But I'm certain that they will be.

We are going to begin in a strange place with the battle of Gog and Magog but I promise you that we will end up back in 2Thessalonians.

There are three battles called "Gog and Magog" in the Bible. We know that Satan is on earth deceiving the nations to attack Israel for two of them. The first battle of Gog and Magog is described in Ezekiel chapter 38 and seems to be forming now in Syria. The second battle of Gog and Magog is described in Ezekiel chapter 39 and will happen at the end of the seven year Tribulation period. Ezekiel 39 describes the same battle as the battle of Armageddon. We know that Satan will empower the Antichrist to oppress Israel during the Tribulation. So Satan is cast out of heaven well before the battle of Armageddon.

Rev 12:13 And when the dragon saw that he was cast unto the earth, he persecuted the woman which brought forth the man child.

The third battle of Gog and Magog is described in Revelation chapter 20 and will happen after Jesus Christ rules on earth for one thousand years. Satan is let out of hell before that battle begins!

Rev 20:7 And when the thousand years are expired, Satan shall be loosed out of his prison,

Every battle of Gog and Magog represents the collective rebellion of the original nations of the old world (primarily the nations from northern Africa to India). These are the Islamic nations of today. Satan will lead these nations against Israel.

So if Satan will be on earth to lead the nations into Israel during two of these battles; then we should expect Satan to be on earth during the first battle of Gog and Magog as well. We should expect Satan to be cast out of heaven and to fall to earth like lightning before Turkey leads the forces that are now fighting in Syria into the Golan Heights of northern Israel!

Jesus said…

Luke 10:18 And he said unto them, I beheld Satan as lightning fall from heaven.

The word that is translated as "lightning" means to *glare* or *shine brightly*. So Jesus is describing a bright shining light rather than a brief flash like that of a lightning bolt.

The fall of Satan is a recurring theme in the Old Testament.

Isaiah 14:12 How art thou fallen from heaven, O Lucifer, son of the morning! how art thou cut down to the ground, which didst weaken the nations!

The King of Tyre is compared to Satan.

Eze 28:17 Thine heart was lifted up because of thy beauty, thou hast corrupted thy wisdom by reason of thy brightness: I will cast thee to the ground, I will lay thee before kings, that they may behold thee.

Yes Satan has fallen from his previous estate as one of God's most glorious angels. BUT Satan is still in heaven.

Jesus said this just before he went to the cross:

John 12:31 Now is the judgment of this world: now shall the prince of this world be cast out.

Two thousand years latter God has not yet judged the world and Satan has not yet been cast out of heaven.

There will be a war in heaven and Satan will be cast out. This happens some time before God establishes his kingdom on earth. We know that Satan will be on earth during the Tribulation period; even before the Tribulation begins. So it is possible that Satan will be cast out of heaven before the Rapture. I think that we will see that happen very soon.

Rev 12:7-12 And there was war in heaven: Michael and his angels fought against the dragon; and the dragon fought and his angels, 8 And prevailed not; neither was their place found any more in heaven. 9 And the great dragon was cast out, that old serpent, called the Devil, and Satan, which deceiveth the whole world: he was cast out into the earth, and his angels were cast out with him. 10 And I heard a loud voice saying in heaven, Now is come salvation, and strength, and the kingdom of our God, and the power of his Christ: for the accuser of our brethren is cast down, which accused them before our God day and night. 11 And they overcame him by the blood of the Lamb, and by the word of their testimony; and they loved not their lives unto the death. 12 Therefore rejoice, ye heavens, and ye that dwell in them. Woe to the inhabiters of the earth and of the sea! for the devil is come down unto you, having great wrath, because he knoweth that he hath but a short time.

Satan had already fallen from his initial state of glory but was still traveling between heaven and earth during the time of Job.

Job 2:1-2 Again there was a day when the sons of God came to present themselves before the LORD, and Satan came also among them to present himself before the LORD. 2 And the LORD said unto Satan, From whence comest thou? And Satan answered the LORD, and said, From going to and fro in the earth, and from walking up and down in it.

We should expect to see a bright shining light in the heavens as Satan hurtles though space towards the earth!

According to 2Thessalonians; two events must happen before the Tribulation begins. These two events are a "falling away" (or the falling of Satan from heaven to earth) and the revealing of the Antichrist with blasphemy against the God of Israel and against his son Jesus Christ, and also with fake miracles

2Thessalonians 2:3 Let no man deceive you by any means: for that day shall not come, except there come a falling away first, and that man of sin be revealed, the son of perdition;

The Christians in Thessalonica were worried that the Rapture had not happened. They thought that the Tribulation had begun. The apostle Paul assured them that the Tribulation had not begun because Satan had not yet fallen from heaven to earth so that he could empower the Antichrist.

When you see the bright shining light hurtling through space towards earth, recognize it as Satan falling. I think that we should expect to see this soon!

Chapter Seventeen

Not so fast with the apostasy

"A falling away" is the casting out of Satan from heaven

By Craig C. White

The Greek word "apostasia" is translated as "a falling away" in 2Thessalonians 2:3 below. Most Christians assume that *apostasia* refers to the apostasy of the Church. But hold on one minute. The word apostasia may have a little different meaning than you first thought. A falling away actually refers to the casting out of Satan from heaven.

2Thessalonians 2:3 Let no man deceive you by any means: for that day shall not come, except there come a falling away first, and that man of sin be revealed, the son of perdition;

The Greek word "apostasia" is used three times in its masculine form in Mat 5:31, Mat 19:7, and Mar 10:4. In these three verses "apostasia" always means "divorce". Apostasia is used twice in its feminine form in Acts 21:21, and 2Th 2:3. It is translated as "forsake" and as "a falling away".

Interestingly the root of the Greek word apostasia comes from these two words.

1) *aphistēmi*, Phonetic: af-is'-tay-mee

Thayer Definition:
to make stand off, cause to withdraw, to remove
to excite to revolt
to stand off, to stand aloof
to go away, to depart from anyone
to desert, withdraw from one
to fall away, become faithless
to shun, flee from
to cease to vex one
to withdraw one's self from, to fall away

59

to keep one's self from, absent one's self from

Strong's Definition:
to remove, that is, (actively) instigate to revolt; usually (reflexively) to desist, desert, etc.: - depart, draw (fall) away, refrain, withdraw self.

And also from this word:

2) *apo*, Phonetic: apo'

Thayer Definition:
of separation
of local separation, after verbs of motion from a place, i.e. of departing, of fleeing,
of separation of a part from the whole
where of a whole some part is taken
of any kind of separation of one thing from another by which the
union or fellowship of the two is destroyed
of a state of separation, that is of distance
physical, of distance of place
temporal, of distance of time
of origin
of the place whence anything is, comes, befalls, is taken
of origin of a cause
Origin: a primary particle

Strong's Definition:
A primary particle; " off", that is, away (from something near), in various senses (of place, time, or relation; literally or figuratively): - (X here-) after, ago, at, because of, before, by (the space of), for (-th), from, in, (out) of, off, (up-) on (-ce), since, with. In composition (as a prefix) it usually denotes separation, departure, cessation, completion, reversal, etc.

So in its most basic form the word *apostasia* means to *actively cause something to be removed away from some place near* Just like God will cause Satan to be removed from heaven.

Now let's think about this. The Apostle Paul gave the early Church two events that must happen before the Tribulation begins. Namely *a falling away first, and that man of sin be revealed.* Since these two events have not yet happened they are also signs to the Church that the Rapture has not yet occurred. If apostasy of the Church is a sign of the Rapture then how do we know when there is enough apostasy? There has always been apostasy in the Christian Church. That isn't much of a sign. Besides, in some parts of the world many people are turning to Christianity. Many Christians are being killed for their faith. These martyrs haven't fallen away from their faith. So the end time must not be near. Not so. The end time is near. It is upon us but the apostasy of the Church isn't the sign.

I don't tell you this because I want to be right. I am telling you because I think that we may all soon witness a bright shining light streaming through space towards earth as Satan is cast out of heaven. As a matter of fact we may witness several bright shining lights streaming through space towards earth as Satan's demons follow. When you see the bright shining light hurtling through space towards earth, recognize it as Satan falling. Know that Jesus will follow closely behind.

Here is something to consider. Ezekiel chapter 38 says that Turkey will lead Iran, Libya, and Sudan into Israel. All of these nations are fighting in Syria now. Jeremiah 49:23 says that the destruction of Damascus will begin at Hamah and Tell Rifaat in northwestern Syria. The Turkish Army is amassed near Hamah and Tell Rifaat now. Turkish President Erdogan is threatening to attack. I think that Turkey will attack northwestern Syria and then march southward to destroy Damascus. Then Turkey will lead the forces that are now fighting in Syria into northern Israel. The Golan Heights are only thirty miles away from Damascus. Nahum chapter 1

61

describes Jesus Christ coming in a fiery whirlwind to the Golan Heights. I think that Jesus will return to cause the Turkish led invaders to retreat when they enter the Golan Heights of Israel. I think that Jesus will collect his Church at that time. I think that Satan must be cast out of heaven before Turkey invades northern Israel.

Chapter Eighteen

Question: What do these Bible verses have in common?

"But of that day and hour knoweth no man" and "one shall be taken, and the other left"

Answer: They have nothing at all to do with the Rapture.

By Craig C. White

Did you know that not a single one of these verses pertains to Church age Christians? I'll bet that you didn't. Every one of these Bible verses are from Matthew chapter 24. Matthew chapter 24 was written directly to the Jews living in and around Jerusalem during the time of their great tribulation. Matthew chapter 24 has nothing at all to do with the Church. Earthquakes are not a sign of the Rapture. The Church is not being warned to be on the lookout for false prophets. God's elect are not Church age believers. A *generation* should not be counted from the date that Israel became a nation until the time of the Rapture. The phrase "But of that day and hour knoweth no man" does not refer to the day of the Rapture! The *days of Noah* do not describe conditions on earth before the Rapture. At the Rapture one shall not be taken, and the other left. The Christians that I talk with don't understand any of these verses. It is High Time that Christians properly understood their Bibles.

In Matthew chapter 24 Jesus is addressing his Jewish disciples. The Gentile Church is still a mystery. Jesus is telling his disciples about the trials that Jerusalem and Judea will endure during their great tribulation.

Matthew 24:3 And as he sat upon the mount of Olives, the disciples came unto him privately, saying, Tell us, when shall these things be? and what shall be the sign of thy coming, and of the end of the world?

Jerusalem's great tribulation will begin during the middle of the seven year long Tribulation period. One day unexpectedly the armies of the Antichrist will attack

Jerusalem and Judea and take half of the people as prisoners. This begins Jerusalem's great tribulation. Some bad things will happen before the Antichrist invades Jerusalem. Jesus warns the Jews living around Jerusalem to be on the lookout for false teachers and also for great wars and natural disasters.

Matthew 24:4-5 And Jesus answered and said unto them, Take heed that no man deceive you. 5 For many shall come in my name, saying, I am Christ; and shall deceive many.

Almost every Christian is tracking earthquakes as a sign of the approaching Rapture. That is a big mistake. Earthquakes, famines, and disease outbreaks are signs to Israel that their day of trouble is near! Earthquakes are not a sign of the Rapture.

Matthew 24:6-8 And ye shall hear of wars and rumours of wars: see that ye be not troubled: for all these things must come to pass, but the end is not yet. 7 For nation shall rise against nation, and kingdom against kingdom: and there shall be famines, and pestilences, and earthquakes, in divers places. 8 All these are the beginning of sorrows.

Almost every Christian sees the Church represented in the following verse. Not so. This verse is talking about the day that the Antichrist invades Jerusalem and captures or kills its inhabitants. From that day the nations will oppress Israel for three and one half years.

Matthew 24:9 Then shall they deliver you up to be afflicted, and shall kill you: and ye shall be hated of all nations for my name's sake.

In the next verse; these false prophets will deceive Israel during their time of trouble. These false prophets are not sent to the Church. These false prophets are already at work in

Israel. They are saying that Israel will have peace and safety if they allow their enemies to share their land.

Matthew 24:11 And many false prophets shall rise, and shall deceive many.

When Matthew chapter 24 mentions the *elect* it is not talking about Christians but it is talking about Israel, God's *chosen* people. The Jewish people must beware of false Christ's as well as false prophets. It seems that Matthew is saying that the false Christs will arise once the great tribulation begins.

Matthew 24:23-24 Then if any man shall say unto you, Lo, here is Christ, or there; believe it not. 24 For there shall arise false Christs, and false prophets, and shall shew great signs and wonders; insomuch that, if it were possible, they shall deceive the very elect.

I know that the following verse sounds like it is describing the Rapture but it isn't. The *elect* identifies Israel, God's *chosen* people not the Church. After the Tribulation, Jesus Christ will collect all of the faithful Jews who have been dispersed throughout the world from the time of Abraham. They won't be taken up into heaven. They will be resurrected and travel back to Israel. Throughout their history the Jewish people have been taken away to places like Egypt, Assyria (northern Iraq), and Babylon (southern Iraq). God will dry up the Red Sea, and the Tigris, and Euphrates Rivers so that the Old Testament Jews can cross over them on their way back to Israel. Please notice that there is no mention of the Jews ascending into the sky.

Matthew 24:31 And he shall send his angels with a great sound of a trumpet, and they shall gather together his elect from the four winds, from one end of heaven to the other.

I have heard so many Christians trying to reconcile the length of a generation in order to establish the timeframe of the Rapture. Wow that is another big mistake. The generation of Jews who see the beginning of the Tribulation will also see the end of the Tribulation and the second coming of Jesus Christ. Try as I may, I cannot correct the thinking of modern day Christians.

Matthew 24:34 Verily I say unto you, This generation shall not pass, till all these things be fulfilled.

Here is a BIG one. Boy how many times have I been rebuked by Christians using this verse? These Christians do not understand their Bibles. The day and hour that Jesus identifies is not the day of the Rapture. It isn't even the day of Jesus Christ's second coming. Jesus is WARNING the Jews living around Jerusalem to WATCH for the armies of the Antichrist as they approach Jerusalem. On that day they are instructed to flee to the mountainous wilderness east of Jerusalem. That day begins Jerusalem's great tribulation. The faithful Jews who heed Jesus' warning will take refuge in Jordan during the great tribulation.

Matthew 24:36 But of that day and hour knoweth no man, no, not the angels of heaven, but my Father only.

Here is another one. The *days of Noah* do not describe the poor spiritual condition on earth today. The *days of Noah* don't even describe the poor spiritual condition on earth before the great tribulation begins. The days of Noah describe the *sudden destruction* that will come upon Jerusalem and Judea when the armies of the Antichrist attack! The point is that this invasion will be a BIG SURPRISE. On a day when everybody in Jerusalem is living their lives as usual then sudden destruction will come upon them just like the flood took Noah's generation by surprise!

Matthew 24:37 But as the days of Noe were, so shall also the coming of the Son of man be.

I hate to burst your fuzzy brain bubble but the next verse does not describe the Rapture of the Church. Matthew is still chronicling the events of the day of Jerusalem's trouble.

When the Antichrist invades Jerusalem, his armies will take one Jew as prisoner and leave the next. In that way one half of the inhabitants of Jerusalem will be taken away captive. This is the same thing that Antiochus Epiphanies did when his armies invaded Jerusalem in 167 BC.

Matthew 24:40 Then shall two be in the field; the one shall be taken, and the other left.

When the Antichrist invades Jerusalem then half of its residents will be taken captive. Zechariah tells us all about it.

Zechariah 14:1-3 Behold, the day of the LORD cometh, and thy spoil shall be divided in the midst of thee. 2 For I will gather all nations against Jerusalem to battle; and the city shall be taken, and the houses rifled, and the women ravished; and half of the city shall go forth into captivity, and the residue of the people shall not be cut off from the city. 3 Then shall the LORD go forth, and fight against those nations, as when he fought in the day of battle.

In the next verse the term "Son of man" does not describe Jesus at his second coming nor does it describe Jesus when he comes for the Church at the Resurrection and Rapture. Believe it or not the term "Son of man" refers to the Antichrist as he approaches Jerusalem.

Matthew 24:44 Therefore be ye also ready: for in such an hour as ye think not the Son of man cometh.

This is the same day that is described in Luke 17:30-31.

Luke 17:30-31 Even thus shall it be in the day when the Son of man is revealed. 31 In that day, he which shall be upon the housetop, and his stuff in the house, let him not come down to take it away: and he that is in the field, let him likewise not return back.

On the day that the armies of the Antichrist attack Jerusalem and Judea its residents are instructed to WATCH and to run for their lives. They must not return home for anything because the Antichrist's armies will be going house to house capturing every other Jew. They must flee into the Judean wilderness in order to escape being captured or killed. It would be nice if Christians finally understood this. I think that the residents of Judea might be interested in knowing.

Chapter Nineteen

Nobody can know!!! Nobody can know!!! Nobody can know!!!

Yes we can know!!!

By Craig C. White

OK folks, here is a typical response that I receive from Christians when I tell them that Turkish President Erdogan is the Antichrist. They generally tell me that "nobody can know". Know what? It seems that Christians believe that nobody can know anything, but that doesn't stop them from instructing you when you say that you do know.

They say something like "Well my Bible says that only The Father knows the time of the second coming".

Many Christians say that nobody can know the time of Jesus Christ's Second Coming. First of all, the Second Coming of Jesus Christ has nothing at all to do with the revealing of the Antichrist. Christians are not looking for the Second Coming. We are looking for the day of the Rapture. The Second Coming of Jesus Christ happens at the end of the Tribulation period when Jesus returns to rescue the nation of Israel from the many nations that have gathered against it. But is that statement even true? Of which day and hour does nobody know?

A lot of Christians point to the following verse and conclude that nobody can know the day of Jesus Christ's Second coming, or that nobody can know the day that Jesus Christ will return to rapture his Church.

Matthew 24:36 But of that day and hour knoweth no man, no, not the angels of heaven, but my Father only.

But which "day" is Jesus referring to? Jesus is not referring to his Second Coming. Jesus is not even referring to the Rapture. Jesus is telling the Jews living around Jerusalem to watch for the Antichrist approaching. The Antichrist along with his armies will enter Jerusalem and capture or kill the Jews living there. This day begins Jerusalem's great tribulation. The Great Tribulation is a three and one half year period that happens during the second half of the seven year long Tribulation period predicted in Daniel 9:27.

Matthew 24:21 For then shall be great tribulation, such as was not since the beginning of the world to this time, no, nor ever shall be.

Jesus warned of great danger in Jerusalem and Judea at a time when its citizens were living their daily lives as usual. He said that it would be like the days of Noah just before the flood. It would be a surprise! He said that life would be going on normally just like in Sodom before God rained fire upon the city. The following verses do not pertain to Church age believers. They are not describing an abundance of sin on earth. They are not describing the days before the Rapture. They do not even refer to Jesus Christ's Second Coming. These verses apply to the region around Jerusalem. It will be life as usual just before the Antichrist makes a surprise attack on Jerusalem and Judea during the middle of the seven year long tribulation period. This begins Jerusalem's Great Tribulation (Mat 24:21).

Luke 17:26-29 And as it was in the days of Noe (Noah), so shall it be also in the days of the Son of man. 27 They did eat, they drank, they married wives, they were given in marriage, until the day that Noe entered into the ark, and the flood came, and destroyed them all. 28 Likewise also as it was in the days of Lot; they did eat, they drank, they bought, they sold, they planted, they builded; 29 But the same day that Lot went out of Sodom it rained fire and brimstone from heaven, and destroyed them all.

So nobody knows the day and time that the Antichrist will attack Jerusalem. Nobody knows because it will be a surprise attack. Jesus instructs the residents of Judea to WATCH!!!

The Bible instructs us to know and to watch so don't allow the idea that "nobody can know" to spoil your viewpoint.

We as Christians are not not looking for Jesus Christ's Second Coming. We are expecting Jesus to return to rescue believers from a terrible time of trouble on earth. The Apostle Paul told us that two events must happen before the Church is rescued (or raptured). Those two things are the falling of Satan from heaven to earth and the revealing of the Antichrist (2 Thessalonians 2:3). Well my friends I am telling you that Turkish President Erdogan is the Antichrist and that the Resurrection and Rapture, and the Tribulation are near. Yes we can know!!!

Chapter Twenty

Bible prophecy is being fulfilled in Mosul

The Prophet Nahum describes the destruction and flooding of Mosul.

By Craig C. White

I am fervently watching events in Mosul. At some point I am expecting Mosul to be destroyed by a flood of water. Mosul is Iraq's second largest city with a pre-war population of nearly two million people. Nearly one million residents have been displaced from their homes.

Mosul is built around the ruins of ancient Nineveh. As a matter of fact Iraqis still refer to Mosul as Nineveh. Nineveh was the capital of the Assyrian Empire. The Assyrians were infamous for committing the same sorts of atrocities that ISIS is known for today. The Prophet Nahum calls them vile. The Prophet Nahum predicted the flooding and plundering of Nineveh. Nineveh was flooded by the Tigris River and then set upon by the Babylonians, Medes, and Persians in 612 BC. The city was plundered and burned for two months until almost nothing remained. Today these same nations are fighting against ISIS in Mosul. Nahum predicted the flooding and destruction of Nineveh but his words could apply to the modern day city of Mosul even more.

Let me begin by saying that the Old Testament book of Nahum definitely predicts that Nineveh (or modern day Mosul) will be destroyed by a flood of water. Remember that ancient Nineveh was flooded in 612 BC.

Nahum 1:8 But with an overrunning flood he will make an utter end of the place thereof, and darkness shall pursue his enemies.

Nahum says that the gates of the Tigris River will be opened. Today the Mosul dam is in danger of bursting. If the Mosul dam broke it could send a seventy five foot tall wave of water over downtown Mosul.

Nahum 2:6 The gates of the rivers shall be opened, and the palace shall be dissolved.

Nahum also says that the palace will be dissolved. Interestingly the palace of Assyrian King Sennacherib has just been rediscovered for the first time since Nineveh was flooded in 612 BC. The palace ruins are located in eastern Mosul directly across the Tigris River from the "Old City" neighborhood which was the last stronghold of ISIS.

Nahum 2:8 But Nineveh is of old like a pool of water: yet they shall flee away. Stand, stand, shall they cry; but none shall look back.

In the verse above, Nahum is saying that Nineveh will look like a water reservoir for many days. So Nahum definitely describes a flood of water, but Nahum also describes an invading army and the defeat of the Assyrian forces by military combat.

Nahum 3:1-3 Woe to the bloody city! it is all full of lies and robbery; the prey departeth not; 2 The noise of a whip, and the noise of the rattling of the wheels, and of the pransing horses, and of the jumping chariots. 3 The horseman lifteth up both the bright sword and the glittering spear: and there is a multitude of slain, and a great number of carcases; and there is none end of their corpses; they stumble upon their corpses:

Nahum 3:3 describes Nineveh as being littered with dead bodies. This week Nahum 3:3 has been fulfilled. The Iraqi Army cannot allow the residents of western Mosul to return to their homes because there are so many dead bodies that must be removed. Even one year later they are still removing corpses from Mosul's Old City neighborhood.

Compare Nahum 3:3 to this quote from this story in the Mirror titled; ISIS' last stand: How bloody final battle for Mosul took place in tiny 150-yard street strewn with bodies.

"Families described not being able to walk without stepping on a corpse or a body part and were holed up with suicide bombers in the tiny street"

The following verse describes Assyrian soldiers as they hide from the advancing army. To seek strength means that they will look for a fortified shelter to protect themselves from the battle.

Nahum 3:11 Thou also shalt be drunken: thou shalt be hid, thou also shalt seek strength because of the enemy.

This week many ISIS fighters have been pulled out of tunnels and out from beneath rubble where they were hiding.

The next verse says that their fortified fighting positions will be readily defeated. The Iraqi Army has made steady progress against ISIS in Mosul; pushing them into a small patch of the Old City neighborhood next to the Tigris River.

Nahum 3:12 All thy strong holds shall be like fig trees with the firstripe figs: if they be shaken, they shall even fall into the mouth of the eater.

Yes I think that the book of Nahum predicts the flooding of ISIS in Mosul, but Nahum also describes the Assyrian Army (and perhaps ISIS as well) as they are killed by fire and by sword. These things have happened in Mosul over the past several months.

Nahum 3:14-15 Draw thee waters for the siege, fortify thy strong holds: go into clay, and tread the morter, make strong the brickkiln. 15 There shall the fire devour thee; the sword shall cut thee off, it shall eat thee up like the cankerworm: make thyself many as the cankerworm, make thyself many as the locusts.

Several events that Nahum describes have already happened in Mosul. Here are a few other things that we can expect to see happen soon that would confirm Nahum's prophecy.

Nahum 1:11 says that a wicked leader will come out of Nineveh. ISIS leader Abu Bakr Al-Baghdadi is thought to have fled Mosul. It is suspected that he is hiding in small ISIS controlled villages west of Mosul.

Nahum 1:11 There is one come out of thee, that imagineth evil against the LORD, a wicked counsellor.

There have been a lot of mixed reports lately about whether or not Al-Baghdadi has been killed. Pentagon chief Jim Mattis said on July 14, 2017 that the US cannot confirm that ISIS leader Al-Baghdadi is dead.

"If we knew, we would tell you — right now, I can't confirm or deny it," Mattis said. "Our approach is we assume he's alive until it's proven otherwise, and right now I can't prove it otherwise."

In the next verse Nahum says that this wicked leader will formally address his troops. So a message from Al-Baghdadi to the last remaining ISIS fighters in Mosul would be appropriate.

Nahum 2:5 He shall recount his worthies: they shall stumble in their walk; they shall make haste to the wall thereof, and the defence shall be prepared.

Nahum 1:10 says that the Assyrians (or perhaps ISIS) will be gathered closely together when they are destroyed. ISIS has been gathered together in western Mosul. In Nahum 1:14 God says that he will punish the people of Nineveh (or Mosul) because they are vile. That certainly describes ISIS. Mosul is Nineveh and ISIS is a revived the Assyrian State. In Nahum 1:9 God says that "affliction shall not rise up the second time." meaning that God will not allow the Assyrian Empire to afflict Israel for a second time. Today we can see ISIS being diminished in Syria and northern Iraq. We are seeing Bible prophecy being fulfilled in Mosul. Be on the lookout for more to follow. At some point expect Mosul to be destroyed by a flood of water.

Chapter Twenty One

Al-Baghdadi addresses ISIS troops just like Nahum predicted

"Oh Soldiers of the Caliphate"

By Craig C. White

The Prophet Nahum makes several predictions concerning Mosul in northern Iraq. Here is the latest one to come to fulfillment.

In the next verse Nahum says that Mosul's wicked leader will formally address his troops just before the city of Mosul is destroyed by a flood of water.

Nahum 2:5 He shall recount his worthies: they shall stumble in their walk; they shall make haste to the wall thereof, and the defence shall be prepared.

ISIS leader Abu Bakr Al-Baghdadi has just released a 46 minute long voice recording addressing his ISIS troops in Iraq and Syria, and around the world. He said...

"Oh Soldiers of the Caliphate, fan the flames of war on your enemies, take it to them and besiege them in every corner, and stand fast and courageous."

"Beware of retreat, or the feeling of defeat, beware of negotiations or surrender. Do not lay down your arms,"

Al- Baghdadi hasn't given a public address since 2016. In Nahum 2:5 the phrase "recount his worthies" means to "bring to remembrance (or to mention) his gallant men". This is exactly what the ISIS leader did in his recorded call to arms. This is exactly the sort of speech that the book of Nahum would lead you to expect.

In the very next verse Nahum describes the flooding of Mosul.

Nahum 2:6 The gates of the rivers shall be opened, and the palace shall be dissolved.

Al- Baghdadi's address is very big news but there is a lot more coming to Mosul. The Prophet Nahum gives us remarkable insight into end time events. Nahum may even describe Jesus Christ as he returns to earth at the Resurrection and Rapture to also do some housecleaning in the Golan Heights as well as in Mosul.

It is evident in his recorded message that ISIS leader al-Baghdadi has Turkey on his mind! Al-Baghdadi said that war between Turkey and the Kurds is "inevitable". I've been saying that for seven years now but nobody is listening. At least al-Baghdadi knows what's going on. I wonder if he reads my books.

The Prophet Jeremiah predicts that Turkey will attack the northwestern Syria cities of Hamah and Tell-Rifaat. Then the residents of Damascus will flee and Damascus will be destroyed. Tell-Rifaat is called Arpad in Jeremiah 49:23.

Jeremiah 49:23 Concerning Damascus. Hamath is confounded, and Arpad: for they have heard evil tidings: they are fainthearted; there is sorrow on the sea; it cannot be quiet.

Hamah and Tell-Rifaat are the two Kurdish towns that the Turkish Army is targeting right now. If you won't believe me then perhaps you will believe Abu Bakr Al-Baghdadi. Turkey will attack northern Syria and then destroy Damascus.

ISIS claims that the Las Vegas shooter was obeying the ISIS leader's recorded message. ISIS says that the Las Vegas shooter converted to Islam a few months ago. In ISIS reports they even call him by his Muslim name. While this is still being investigated; there is some reason to believe that this is true.

The Prophet Nahum predicted the ISIS leader's message so we had better pay attention. In his message Al-Baghdadi tells his troops to rise up against the West as well as against Christians and the Kurds.

Al-Baghdadi said...

"Continue your jihad and blessed operations, and do not let the Crusaders and apostates enjoy a good life or a pleasant living in the middle of their countries while your brothers are experiencing bombardment, killing, and destruction,"

ISIS often refers to Americans and all westerners as *crusaders*.

Over the past couple of years there has been an all-out war on ISIS in Iraq and Syria. Al-Baghdadi knows that his time is almost up. Al-Baghdadi's message is a last ditch attempt to do harm.

Recent terrorist attacks in Canada and France are being cited as being responses to Al-Baghdadi's recorded message. More attacks are expected in response to the ISIS leader's call to arms to all ISIS fighters. It seems that Al-Baghdadi's recorded message will not be without consequence. Be alert to the possibility of more terror attacks.

Let me leave you with this. The Prophet Nahum predicts one last ISIS stand in Mosul and also the flooding of the city. We should probably expect another message from Al-Baghdadi telling all ISIS members to retake Mosul. I wish that Christians were more alert to the biblical events of the day.

Chapter Twenty Two

2018 Bible Prophecy Timeline

Copyright 2017 Craig C. White

We can see Jesus coming!

By Craig C. White

2018 is upon us and end time Bible prophecy is becoming clearer and clearer to see. Every year I tell you that these end time events typically take longer than I suspect to come to pass. Now it seems that Bible events are cued up and ready to begin in earnest. I think that Jesus will return within the next couple of years.

The path to Jesus Christ's return for his Church is easy to see! The nearer that the Turkish Army gets to Israel, the nearer that Jesus will get to Israel, and the nearer that Christians will get to being rescued. Unfortunately that means that seven years of God's wrath is about to begin for Israel and also for the rest of the world.

The Prophet Jeremiah told us about two northwestern Syria cities that will hear evil reports just before the residents of Damascus flee and then Damascus is destroyed. So the invaders that destroy Damascus will come from the north. Jeremiah 49:23 identifies Hamah and Arpad (or modern day Tell Rifaat). The Turkish Army is amassed near both of these cities now. Turkish President Erdogan is threatening to attack the Kurds in Hamah and Tell Rifaat. Erdogan has also promised to remove Syrian President Assad from power in Damascus. Erdogan said that the sole reason that Turkey has entered Syria is to remove Assad.

By the way, Turkish President Erdogan is the Antichrist; scout's honor. Just a side note: we should expect to see Satan being cast out of heaven and falling to the earth soon. This will become apparent as Satan empowers Turkish President Erdogan to blaspheme the God of Israel and to perform false

High Time to Awake – 2018 Bible Prop

The nearer that Turkey gets to Israel, the nearer that Jesus will get to Israel. Turkish President Erdogan is the Antichrist. Erdogan is the "chief prince" or primary governor among the provinces of Turkey mentioned in Ezekiel 38. Jeremiah 49:23 mentions two northwestern Syria cities that will hear evil reports just before the destruction of Damascus. Those two cities are Hamah and Arpad (or Tell-Rifaat). The Turkish Army is amassed near both of these cities right now. Erdogan has vowed to remove Syrian President Assad from power. The next thing that will happen is the attack on Hamah and Tell-Rifaat and the destruction of Damascus. Then Turkey will lead the forces that are fighting in Syria into the Golan Heights of Israel (Ezekiel 38) only thirty miles away from Damascus. I would expect to see Jesus Christ at that time!

Turkey threatens Hamah & Tell Rifaat	Satan falls from heaven	Fethullah Gulen reconciles with Erdogan	ISIS fl in M
Residents of Damascus flee	empowers Erdogan	Head of Ottoman Empire is healed	Perha Jesus (per
Jer 49:23-24	2Thes 2:1-17	Rev 13:3	Nahum

2018 ———————————————————————————— **2019**

Turkey destroys Damascus	Al-Baghdadi rallies ISIS for final uprising in Mosul	Battle of Gog and Magog
Installs Muslim Brotherhood ruler		Turkey leads Iran, Sudan, and Libya into the Golan Heights of Israel
Jer 49:25, Isa 17:1	Nahum 2:5	Eze 38:1-6

A lot of Bible prophecy that was written about Nineveh has already been ISIS leader Al-Baghdadi recently recorded a message to his troops. His messa Nahum 2:5-6 which predicts one last ISIS uprising in Mosul and the flooding book of Nahum also describes the coming in the air of Jesus Christ!!! Nahum pass by the Golan Heights and burn the ground with the heat of his furious an 38 describes a Turkish led invasion into the Golan Heights of Israel. I expect happen after Turkey destroys Damascus. Turkish President Erdogan said that could come *suddenly and all at once*. I suspect that Jesus Christ will judge M he comes for his Church! Jesus will also fight against the Turkish led forces o

miracles. It could be that Satan will enrage Turkish President Erdogan to finally attack Israel.

A lot of Bible prophecy that was written about the ancient Assyrian capital city of Nineveh has already been fulfilled in Mosul. The northern Iraq city of Mosul is built around the

ophecy Timeline – hightimetoawake.com

Jesus is in sight! It is easy to identify and to watch the events that lead up to Jesus' return. As Turkey and their allies move nearer and nearer to Israel we can know that Jesus is on his way. Jesus will return to turn back the Turkish led invaders on the Golan Heights and to take his Church away. Afterwards I think that a peace deal will be made beginning the seven year Tribulation period.

Today the Turkish Army is threating to attack Hamah and Tell-Rifaat. I've been telling you about these end time events for the past seven years and now we can see them happening; so I suggest that you receive my words and confirm them according to the scriptures.

IS flooded in Mosul	The Rapture	Turkey conquers Egypt installs its fierce king.
erhaps by us Christ in person	Jesus Christ gives the order to gather Church age believers. The dead in Christ are resurrected first	Morsi reinstated as President of Egypt
hum 1:8, 2:6	1Th 4:16, Psalm 50:5	Isaiah 19:4b

RAPTURE   T R I B U L A T I O N

gog dan, lan	Jesus Christ returns in the air to fight on the Golan Heights!	Turkey & Israel seven year Peace Treaty	Russian Union forms with nations on western border
	Nahum 1:3-8	Provision for Jerusalem Temple	Dan 7:5
een fulfilled in Mosul.		Islamic Union forms	
essage is mentioned in		Dan 9:27	Dan 7:6
ding of the city. The		Exodus 23:32-33	

hum says that Jesus will
s anger. Ezekiel chapter
ect this invasion to
that the Turkish Army
e Mosul in person when
es on the Golan Heights.

This timeline is meant to give the reader an idea of upcoming prophetic events. We do not know the specific dates of these events. In my experience these events typically take longer than I suspect. So the order shown may be more accurate than the timing.
© 2017 Craig C. White
hightimetoawake.com

ruins of Nineveh. The Prophet Nahum predicts that an army will attack and destroy Mosul. Last year the Iraqi Army hunted down ISIS fighters street by street until much of Mosul was reduced to ruins. Nahum also predicts a final ISIS uprising in Mosul as well as the flooding of the city.

Most Bible teachers completely ignore the Old Testament book of Nahum but it turns out that Nahum gives us remarkable insight into end time events. The Prophet Nahum makes several other predictions concerning Mosul in northern Iraq. Here is the latest one to come to fulfillment.

In the next verse Nahum says that Mosul's wicked leader will formally address his troops just before a final battle is staged.

Nahum 2:5 He shall recount his worthies: they shall stumble in their walk; they shall make haste to the wall thereof, and the defence shall be prepared.

In September 2017 ISIS leader Abu Bakr Al-Baghdadi released a 46 minute long voice recording addressing his ISIS troops in Iraq and Syria and around the world. Al-Baghdadi told ISIS soldiers in Iraq and Syria to keep fighting. He also told ISIS sympathizers around the world to commit terrorist acts against the west. Now it could be that we will be hearing even more from the ISIS leader.

In the very next verse the city of Mosul is destroyed by a flood of water.

Nahum 2:6 The gates of the rivers shall be opened, and the palace shall be dissolved.

Besides telling us about the destruction and flooding of ancient Nineveh; the book of Nahum also describes the coming in the air of Jesus Christ!!! He comes in a whirlwind and he is HOT!!!

Nahum 1:3-8 The LORD is slow to anger, and great in power, and will not at all acquit the wicked: the LORD hath his way in the whirlwind and in the storm, and the clouds are the dust of his feet. 4 He rebuketh the sea, and maketh it dry, and drieth up all the rivers: Bashan languisheth, and Carmel, and the flower of Lebanon languisheth. 5 The mountains quake at him, and the hills melt, and the earth is burned at his presence, yea, the

world, and all that dwell therein. 6 Who can stand before his indignation? and who can abide in the fierceness of his anger? his fury is poured out like fire, and the rocks are thrown down by him. 7 The LORD is good, a strong hold in the day of trouble; and he knoweth them that trust in him. 8 But with an overrunning flood he will make an utter end of the place thereof, and darkness shall pursue his enemies.

In the verses above, Nahum identifies Bashan, Carmel, and Lebanon. These places all describe the Golan Heights that separate Israel from Syria and Lebanon. So it seems that Jesus Christ will scorch the ground as he passes by the Golan Heights when he comes in the air! But notice that God also protects those people who *trust in him*. This could refer to the Resurrection and Rapture of Church age believers.

Ezekiel chapter 38 describes a Turkish led invasion into the Golan Heights of Israel. I expect this invasion to happen after Turkey attacks Hamah and Tell-Rifaat in northwestern Syria, and then marches southward to destroy Damascus. Every nation that is listed in Ezekiel 38:5 is now fighting in Syria.

Ezekiel 38:20 says that, "all the men that are upon the face of the earth, shall shake at my presence". So it seems that Jesus Christ will fight against the Turkish led invaders in person. Ezekiel says that God will cause these invaders to retreat.

Psalm 50:3-5 describes a similar scenario. Jesus will come in the air in a fiery tornado. Jesus will cause the armies that have gathered against Israel on the Golan Heights to retreat and he will also gather Christians.

Psalm 50:3-5 Our God shall come, and shall not keep silence: a fire shall devour before him, and it shall be very tempestuous round about him. 4 He shall call to the heavens from above, and to the earth, that he may judge his people. 5 Gather my saints together unto me; those that have made a covenant with me by sacrifice.

The Rapture fuse is lit! The nearer that Turkey gets to Israel, the nearer that Jesus will get to Israel.

Turkish President Erdogan is the Antichrist. He will destroy Damascus and then invade the Golan Heights. Jesus will return to turn the Turkish led invaders back and also to take away Christians. Afterwards I think that a peace deal will be made beginning the seven year long Tribulation period.

Chapter Twenty Three

Patterns and Paths Map

Copyright 2018 Craig C. White

of five end time battles

By Craig C. White

God is pretty smart. He wants to teach us about end time events. So God has patterned world history to reflect events that we can now expect to see happen.

I want to point out five paths that are designated by arrows and dots on the Patterns and Paths map.

First look at the black dots labeled as "**1**"; they represent the path that the Turkish Army will follow on their way to destroy Damascus and then invade Israel. Turkey will begin their warpath by harassing the northwestern Syria cities of Hamah and Tell Rifaat. The Turkish Army is amassing near Hamah and Tell Rifaat now. Jeremiah 49:23-27 is all about the Turkish Army as they march from northwestern Syria southward to destroy Damascus. In Jeremiah 49:23 below, the city of Tell Rifaat is called *Arpad*.

Jeremiah 49:23 Concerning Damascus. Hamath is confounded, and Arpad: for they have heard evil tidings: they are fainthearted; there is sorrow on the sea; it cannot be quiet.

After Turkey destroys Damascus they will then lead the forces that are now fighting in Syria into the Golan Heights of Israel. Ezekiel chapter 38 describes Turkey as they lead Iran, Sudan, and Libya in an invasion into Israel. In the next verse Persia is called Iran today and the Hebrew word that is translated as "Ethiopia" is really the name *Cush*. Cush settled in the land south of Egypt. The major nation that is located south of Egypt today is Sudan.

PATTERNS AND PATHS
OF FIVE END TIME BATTLES

Turkey invades Hamah and Arpad (Tell Rifaat) in northwestern Syria, destroys Damascus, then leads the forces that are fighting in Syria into the Golan Heights of northern Israel. (Same path as Assyrian conquest of Syria and invasion of northern Israel 734 BC)

Jesus comes in the air to turn back the Turkish led invaders on the Golan Heights of northern Israel, then floods Mosul, and gathers Christians in the Resurrection and Rapture. (Same path as Jonah)

Mid Tribulation invasion of Jerusalem and Judea by the Antichrist (Same path as Antiochus Epiphanes 167 BC)

Second Coming of Jesus Christ at the end of the Tribulation. Jesus will save the Jewish refugees in Jordan first (Psalm 83) and then enter Jerusalem from the east. (Same path as the Exodus)

Ezekiel 38:5 Persia, Ethiopia, and Libya with them; all of them with shield and helmet:

This is known as the battle of Gog and Magog. Ezekiel chapter 39 describes another battle called Gog and Magog. That battle is the same as the battle of Armageddon and happens at the end of the Tribulation. But every nation that is

90

listed in Ezekiel chapter 38 is now fighting in Syria. So we can expect the first battle of Gog and Magog to happen after Turkey destroys Damascus.

The Turkish conquest of Syria and the following invasion into northern Israel follows along the same path as the Assyrian conquest of Syria and subsequent invasion of northern Israel in 734 BC. The Assyrian attack is a model for the Turkish attack that is now forming in Syria!

Next let's talk about the path represented by the white dots that are labeled as "**2**". After Turkey destroys Damascus then I think that they will lead the forces that are fighting in Syria into the Golan Heights of Israel. The Golan Heights are located just thirty miles south of Damascus.

Nahum 1:4 describes Jesus Christ as he passes over the Golan Heights. As he passes he will burn the ground with a fiery heat.

Nahum 1:4 He rebuketh the sea, and maketh it dry, and drieth up all the rivers: Bashan languisheth, and Carmel, and the flower of Lebanon languisheth.

The book of Nahum is mostly about the destruction and flooding of ancient Nineveh. Today Nineveh is called Mosul in northern Iraq. Mosul is the hometown and headquarters of ISIS. I think that when the Turkish Army reaches the Golan Heights that then Jesus will return in the air to turn back the armies that Turkey has led into northern Israel. Next Jesus will travel to Mosul to flood the city and judge the ISIS fighters that have gathered there for one last rebellion.

This is the same path that Jonah took to Nineveh. Jesus promised the religious leaders of his day that he would give them the sign of Jonah (Mat 12:39). So the coming of Jesus in the air and the flooding of Mosul may be the one sign to Israel before their tribulation begins that Jesus is truly their Messiah. As we will see, the Resurrection and Rapture of gentile believers may also be part of the sign of Jonah!

Nahum also says that Jesus will save those people who trust in him.

Nahum 1:7 The LORD is good, a strong hold in the day of trouble; and he knoweth them that trust in him.

So Jesus is coming in the air in heat and fury. He will pass over the Golan Heights and then travel to Mosul in northern Iraq. I think that while Jesus dispenses his wrath against Israel's enemies he will also gather Christians in the Resurrection and Rapture. Yes that's what I said. The Rapture will happen when the Turkish Army reaches the Golan Heights of Israel! They are in Syria now and headed towards Damascus and then on to Israel.

Now on to the dark gray path that is labeled as "**3**"; during the middle of the seven year long Tribulation period the armies of the Antichrist will launch a surprise attack on Jerusalem and Judea. The attack will come from Egypt.

In Matthew chapter 24 the residents of Jerusalem and Judea are instructed to watch for the coming invasion and to flee into the desert wilderness east of Jerusalem. If the residents of Judea do not watch then they will be killed or be taken away suddenly just like the wicked inhabitants of the earth were taken away by Noah's flood.

Guess what; the mid-Tribulation attack on Jerusalem and Judea is also patterned for us in ancient history. In 167 BC the army of Antiochus Epiphanes suddenly attacked Jerusalem from Egypt. The attack was devastating with many Jews being killed. Antiochus instructed his soldiers to take every other Jew away captive as slaves. In that way *one Jew was taken and the other Jew was left* in Jerusalem. Matthew chapter 24 tells us that the same thing will happen when the Antichrist invades Jerusalem and Judea beginning three and one half years of Jerusalem's great tribulation.

Matthew 24:40-41 Then shall two be in the field; the one shall be taken, and the other left. 41 Two women shall be grinding at the mill; the one shall be taken, and the other left.

Now let's talk about the path that is represented by the light gray dots that are labeled as "**4**" on our map. I think that this is the path that Jesus will follow when he returns at his second coming. This is the same path that Israel took when they left Egypt. If you will remember, Israel was led by a pillar of cloud and fire. So God himself determined Israel's route of travel. This foretold Jesus Christ's own route when he returns to defeat Israel's enemies leading up to the battle of Armageddon.

I would like to point out that the Psalm 83 war will take place in Jordan at the end of the Tribulation period. This is part of Jesus Christ's yellow path of vengeance. Jesus will rescue the Jewish refugees living in Jordan before he enters Jerusalem. Psalm 83 is a cry for God's help by the Jews who have fled from Judea (the region around Jerusalem) when they saw the armies of the Antichrist approaching Jerusalem. The Bible says that the residents of Judea must flee when they see a sign in the temple called *the abomination of desolation.*

Mark 13:14 But when ye shall see the abomination of desolation, spoken of by Daniel the prophet, standing where it ought not, (let him that readeth understand,) then let them that be in Judaea flee to the mountains:

The residents of Judea will take refuge in the Moab region of Jordan for three and one half years. At the end of that time Jordan, Lebanon, and northern Iraq will conspire together to finally eliminate the last remaining enclave of Jews.

Finally the Battle of Armageddon is represented by one gray arrow labeled as "**5**" on the Patterns and Paths map. The arrow begins in the *valley of Megiddo* (that's what Armageddon means) in northern Israel and ends near the Dead Sea. Revelation says that the blood of Israel's enemies will flow for this entire length.

Revelation 14:20 And the winepress was trodden without the city, and blood came out of the winepress, even unto the horse bridles, by the space of a thousand and six hundred furlongs.

You see, at his second coming Jesus will first save the Jewish refugees living in Jordan (spoken of in Psalm 83) and then he will save Jerusalem. Jesus will then travel outside of the city of Jerusalem to trample Israel's enemies like grapes.

Here is the prayer of the Jewish refugees living in Jordan during the second half of the Tribulation. They are asking God to defeat Israel's enemies just like Gideon did long ago. The following verses describe the armies that were destroyed by the Israeli Army while led by Gideon (Judges 4 & 8). The bloodshed of these battles started in the valley of Megiddo and ended in western Jordan near the Dead Sea.

Psalm 83:9 Do unto them as *unto* the Midianites; as *to* Sisera, as *to* Jabin, at the brook of Kison: 10 *Which* perished at Endor: they became *as* dung for the earth. 11 Make their nobles like Oreb, and like Zeeb: yea, all their princes as Zebah, and as Zalmunna: 12 Who said, Let us take to ourselves the houses of God in possession. 13 O my God, make them like a wheel; as the stubble before the wind. 14 As the fire burneth a wood, and as the flame setteth the mountains on fire; 15 So persecute them with thy tempest, and make them afraid with thy storm. 16 Fill their faces with shame; that they may seek thy name, O LORD. 17 Let them be confounded and troubled for ever; yea, let them be put to shame, and perish: 18 That *men* may know that thou, whose name alone *is* JEHOVAH, *art* the most high over all the earth.

The Psalm 83 refugees are asking God to defeat Israel's enemies beginning in the valley of Megiddo. Jesus Christ will answer their prayer personally as he tramples out the vintage of the blood of his enemies outside of the city of Jerusalem from Megiddo to the Dead Sea! This passage proves that the Psalm 83 rescue of Judean refugees in Jordan will happen just before the battle of Armageddon.

Turkey is in position to begin their march to Damascus and then on to the Golan Heights. I think that Jesus will return to cause them to retreat. At that time Jesus will also collect his Church. There is a terrible time coming upon Israel and also upon *all the world*! Jesus is coming soon!

Chapter Twenty Four

Ezekiel 38 and 39 do not cover the invasion of Jerusalem

There will be four separate invasions into Israel. Turkey will lead an invasion into the Golan Heights before the Tribulation. Turkey will overrun Jerusalem during the middle of the Tribulation. Turkey will lead many nations into Israel at end of the Tribulation. These nations will once again come against Israel at the end of the millennial reign of Jesus.

By Craig C. White

Ezekiel chapter 38 and 39 do not cover the mid-Tribulation invasion of Jerusalem by the Antichrist. The three battles of Gog and Magog that are described in Ezekiel chapter 38, Ezekiel chapter 39, and in Revelation 20:8 are all about Turkey as it leads the nations from the four corners of the old world into Israel.

Ezekiel chapter 38 tells us that God will use the forces of nature against Turkey, Iran, Libya, and Sudan to cause them to retreat. It could be that Jesus will return in person to fight against these invaders and also to collect his Church. I think that the Ezekiel chapter 38 invasion will happen in the Golan Heights. Iran, Libya, and Sudan have all been fighting from time to time in the Golan Heights of Syria over the past few years.

The Ezekiel chapter 39 invasion into Israel is the same as the battle of Armageddon that happens at the end of the Tribulation period. Jesus will return at his second coming to defeat the armies that have gathered against Israel.

At the end of the millennial rule of Jesus Christ, Satan will be loosed from hell. Turkey will once again lead the nations against Israel.

The mid-Tribulation invasion of Jerusalem is not described in Ezekiel chapters 38 and 39. The mid-Tribulation invasion of Judea and Jerusalem by the Antichrist is one of the MAJOR themes that Jesus Christ taught in the Gospels. This invasion is modeled after the 167 BC invasion by Antiochus Epiphanies (Dan 8:9-11). Turkey along with Sudan and Libya will enter Israel from Egypt to go house to house taking every other Jew as prisoner. In that way, one shall be taken and the other left. Jerusalem will be overrun by its enemies for three and one half years.

Chapter Twenty Five

Jesus will fight on the Golan Heights!

Image credit: Whirlwind by janeblue329 (modified)
www.flickr.com

Jesus will be HOT when he comes for his Church

By Craig C. White

OK, here is something that you have never considered. The book of Nahum predicts the flooding and destruction of ancient Nineveh. That happened in 612 BC. Today Nineveh is called Mosul in northern Iraq. Mosul is the hometown and headquarters of ISIS. Nahum's prophecy seems to also apply to Mosul today. A lot of Nahum's prophecy has already been fulfilled in Mosul.

Now that isn't even the most curious thing about the book of Nahum. Besides telling us about the destruction and flooding of ancient Nineveh; the book of Nahum also describes the coming of Jesus Christ in the air!!! Jesus comes in a whirlwind and he is HOT!

Nahum 1:3-8 The LORD is slow to anger, and great in power, and will not at all acquit the wicked: the LORD hath his way in the whirlwind and in the storm, and the clouds are the dust of his feet. 4 He rebuketh the sea, and maketh it dry, and drieth up all the rivers: Bashan languisheth, and Carmel, and the flower of Lebanon languisheth. 5 The mountains quake at him, and the hills melt, and the earth is burned at his presence, yea, the world, and all that dwell therein. 6 Who can stand before his indignation? and who can abide in the fierceness of his anger? his fury is poured out like fire, and the rocks are thrown down by him. 7 The LORD is good, a strong hold in the day of trouble; and he knoweth them that trust in him. 8 But with an overrunning flood he will make an utter end of the place thereof, and darkness shall pursue his enemies.

The land around Jesus will melt and burn. In the verses above, Nahum identifies Bashan, Carmel, and Lebanon. These places all describe the Golan Heights that separate Israel from Syria and Lebanon. The book of Nahum begins with God's judgement in the Golan Heights and ends in Nineveh (or today's Mosul in northern Iraq). This is the same path that Jonah followed when God sent him to preach to Nineveh. Jesus promised to give Israel one sign. That is the sign of Jonah.

Ezekiel chapter 38 describes a Turkish led invasion into the Golan Heights of Israel. I expect this invasion to happen after Turkey attacks Hamah and Tell-Rifaat (Tell Rifaat is called *Arpad* in Jeremiah 49:23) in northwestern Syria, and then marches southward to destroy Damascus (Jeremiah 49:23-27). Turkey is preparing to attack these two Syrian cities right now. Turkish President Erdogan said that the Turkish Army could come at *any night suddenly and all at once*. So the Turkish led invasion into the Golan Heights is not far off.

Speaking of fire; I've always wondered where the fire and brimstone would come from in Ezekiel chapter 38. It seems that it will be stirred up by the heat of Jesus' coming. Ezekiel says that God will cause the Turkish led armies to retreat.

Ezekiel 38:22-23 And I will plead against him with pestilence and with blood; and I will rain upon him, and upon his bands, and upon the many people that are with him, an overflowing rain, and great hailstones, fire, and brimstone. 23 Thus will I magnify myself, and sanctify myself; and I will be known in the eyes of many nations, and they shall know that I am the LORD.

Guess what peeps. I think that this next passage refers to Jesus Christ's coming for his Church. The passage precedes a description of Israel's time of trouble. I think that when Jesus collects believers he will be angry with the unbelieving nations, especially those situated around Israel. Jesus won't come floating down sweetly on a fluffy cloud. He will come in a whirlwind. Fire shall devour before him. He will give the order to collect all of the people who have accepted his own sacrifice for sin; namely Jesus Christ's death on a cross.

Psalm 50:3-5 Our God shall come, and shall not keep silence: a fire shall devour before him, and it shall be very tempestuous round about him. 4 He shall call to the heavens from above, and to the earth, that he may judge his people. 5 Gather my saints together unto me; those that have made a covenant with me by sacrifice.

So when Jesus comes for his Church the heat of his coming will scorch the ground where Israel's enemies have gathered. It seems that Jesus will personally fight against the Turkish led invaders who have gathered on the Golan Heights.

A lot of Nahum's prophecy has already been fulfilled in Mosul. Nahum tells us about a final ISIS uprising and the flooding of Mosul yet to come. Jesus Christ may judge Mosul in person when he comes to gather his Church before the Tribulation on earth begins. Jesus will also fight against

101

the Turkish led forces on the Golan Heights. Keep your eye on Mosul but also watch Hamah, Tell Rifaat, Damascus, and the Golan Heights!

Chapter Twenty Six

Creation the universal language

Everybody understands that there is a God

By Craig C. White

The sky proclaims that a glorious God has made it. Its message requires no translation. Every language understands.

Psalm 19:1-3 To the chief Musician, A Psalm of David. The heavens declare the glory of God; and the firmament sheweth his handywork. 2 Day unto day uttereth speech, and night unto night sheweth knowledge. 3 There is no speech nor language, where their voice is not heard.

Every person understands that God exists even if they don't acknowledge him. The overwhelming proof of creation leaves no room for an excuse not to worship God.

Romans 1:20 For the invisible things of him from the creation of the world are clearly seen, being understood by the things that are made, even his eternal power and Godhead; so that they are without excuse:

God created the heavens and the earth and all things in them.

Psalm 33:6-9 By the word of the LORD were the heavens made; and all the host of them by the breath of his mouth. 7 He gathereth the waters of the sea together as an heap: he layeth up the depth in storehouses. 8 Let all the earth fear the LORD: let all the inhabitants of the world stand in awe of him. 9 For he spake, and it was done; he commanded, and it stood fast.

Jesus is God. Jesus existed before he was born as a man. Jesus created all things.

John 1:3 All things were made by him; and without him was not any thing made that was made.

Jesus Christ is God. He came into the world that he created. God came into the world as a man. The world rejected their creator. But to all who receive him he will give friendship and eternal life.

John 1:10-13 He was in the world, and the world was made by him, and the world knew him not. 11 He came unto his own, and his own received him not. 12 But as many as received him, to them gave he power to become the sons of God, even to them that believe on his name: 13 Which were born, not of blood, nor of the will of the flesh, nor of the will of man, but of God.

The people in the world that God made killed Jesus. But God raised Jesus alive from the dead. Death has been overcome by Jesus own death and resurrection. Even after death God has the power to restore life. Jesus has the power to give you everlasting life.

Romans 10:9 That if thou shalt confess with thy mouth the Lord Jesus, and shalt believe in thine heart that God hath raised him from the dead, thou shalt be saved.

You already understand that God created the heavens and the earth. It's time to acknowledge him. Believe that Jesus is God and be saved.

Chapter Twenty Seven

The Holy Spirit in us is our assurance of salvation

and also of our resurrection and new life!

By Craig C. White

When we believe and submit ourselves to God then he gives each open heart the Holy Spirit. The Holy Spirit in us is our promise (our engagement ring) that we will be raised to everlasting life. The Holy Spirit in us is our assurance that we are saved. The Holy Spirit does a few things while it is in our hearts. It convicts us of sin. The Holy Spirit helps us to understand the Bible when we read it or hear it. The Holy Spirit also communicates God's prayers to us so that we can pray in agreement. I have the Holy Spirit in my heart so I am certain that I am saved!

Ephesians 1:13 In whom ye also trusted, after that ye heard the word of truth, the gospel of your salvation: in whom also after that ye believed, ye were sealed with that holy Spirit of promise,

The Bible says that when we are saved God places his *seal* on us in order to identify us as belonging to him, and also to preserve us so that we are guaranteed to receive future promises.

Here is the definition of the word "sealed" in Ephesians 1:13.

sfrag-id'-zo; to stamp (with a signet or private mark) for security or preservation (literally or figuratively); by implication to keep secret, to attest: - (set a, set to) seal up, stop.

God's promise is a pledge to give life more abundantly. When we receive God's Holy Spirit we also receive part of God's gift. But with God a promise made is a promise kept because God will completely fulfill his promise in the future. We will be raised from death to live in joy forever. Or if we are lucky, our bodies will be changed from corruptible to everlasting in the twinkling of an eye.

Here is the definition of the word "promise" in Ephesians 1:13.

ep-ang-el-ee'-ah; an announcement (for information, assent or pledge; especially a divine assurance of good): - message, promise.

Ephesians 1:14 Which is the earnest of our inheritance until the redemption of the purchased possession, unto the praise of his glory.

Here is the definition of the word "earnest" in Ephesians 1:14.

ar-hrab-ohn'; a pledge, that is, part of the purchase money or property given in advance as security for the rest: - earnest.

The word that is translated as "earnest" means *down payment* or *security deposit.* So the Holy Spirit inside of our hearts is our individual assurance that God will keep his promise to us. In Modern Greek the word *arrabona* means an *engagement ring.* Remember that each believer *receives* an engagement ring when they receive the Holy Spirit. If the marriage is called off then you still get to keep the ring! But don't worry; this engagement ring was purchased at great cost. God has assured us that the Holy Spirit will not be given in vain. The wedding will take place as planned.

God calls you and me "the purchased possession". Here is the definition of the term "purchased possession" in Ephesians 1:14.

per-ee-poy'-ay-sis; acquisition (the act or the thing); by extension preservation: - obtain (-ing), peculiar, purchased, possession, saving.

We are purchased possessions because we have been bought with a price (1Corinthians 6:20). Jesus made the payment of sin for us. The penalty for sin is death. Jesus died on the cross so we wouldn't have to die for our sins.

I am certain that I will live forever with Jesus because I have the Holy Spirit in my heart. I know that the Holy Spirit is there because I am ashamed when I sin. I also know that that the Holy Spirit is in my heart because I can understand the Bible when I read it. Believe it or not, sometimes I can even sense what the Holy Spirit is communicating with my spirit. Believe that Jesus Christ died to pay the penalty for your sins and be saved. Open your heart to God's Holy Spirit and receive assurance of everlasting life.

More from High Time to Awake

God's Great Expectations is about God's desire to know us, and about the ramifications of knowing him or rejecting him. It will challenge and inform every Christian. It answers the question "who can be saved?" It also contains an in-depth definition of hell in the bible, and a map of heaven! In "God's Great Expectations" I cover Jesus' claims to be God, as well as the Rapture of the Church.

www.hightimetoawake.com

Chapter Twenty Eight

The times of the Gentiles

The fullness of the Gentiles

By Craig C. White

The times of the Gentiles in Luke 21:24 should not be confused with the fullness of the Gentiles in Romans 11:25.

The "times of the Gentiles" is the period when the nations will have power over Israel. The *times of the Gentiles* will end at Jesus' second coming. In the following verse the Jews will suffer when the Antichrist attacks Jerusalem.

Luke 21:24 And they shall fall by the edge of the sword, and shall be led away captive into all nations: and Jerusalem shall be trodden down of the Gentiles, until the times of the Gentiles be fulfilled.

On the other hand, "the fullness of the Gentiles" refers to the number of people from all nations who will trust in the saving work of Jesus Christ on the cross. After *whosoever will* comes to Jesus then Israel's eyes will be opened to recognize that Jesus Christ truly is their Messiah.

Romans 11:25 For I would not, brethren, that ye should be ignorant of this mystery, lest ye should be wise in your own conceits; that blindness in part is happened to Israel, until the fulness of the Gentiles be come in.

Both of these events will most likely occur when Jesus Christ returns to rescue Israel at his second coming.

Zechariah 12:10 And I will pour upon the house of David, and upon the inhabitants of Jerusalem, the spirit of grace and of supplications: and they shall look upon me whom they have pierced, and they shall mourn for him, as one mourneth for his only son, and shall be in bitterness for him, as one that is in bitterness for his firstborn.

Chapter Twenty Nine

When will Elijah come?

Before the great and dreadful day of the LORD.

By Craig C. White

The Prophet Malachi promises that God will send the Prophet Elijah to Israel before the great and dreadful day of the LORD. So then we must determine when the "day of the LORD" will happen.

The word "day" in Malachi 4:5 tends to refer to a specific day rather than a period of time, so I would suspect that this is the day that Jesus returns to wipe out Israel's enemies.

Malachi 4:5-6 Behold, I will send you Elijah the prophet before the coming of the great and dreadful day of the LORD: 6 And he shall turn the heart of the fathers to the children, and the heart of the children to their fathers, lest I come and smite the earth with a curse.

The Prophet Daniel foretells a coming seven year period of trouble for the nation of Israel. It is referred to as the Tribulation period. The seven years long Tribulation happens just before Jesus returns to judge the nations that have gathered against the nation of Israel.

Yes the nation of Israel will turn to God during the Tribulation period or at least during the second half of the Tribulation called Jerusalem's *great tribulation* in Matthew 24:21.

So when is the "day of the LORD"? Every verse in the Old Testament that refers to "the day of the LORD" describes the day that Jesus will return to judge the nations.

Jeremiah 46:10 For this is the day of the Lord GOD of hosts, a day of vengeance, that he may avenge him of his adversaries: and the sword shall devour, and it shall be satiate and made drunk with their blood: for the Lord

GOD of hosts hath a sacrifice in the north country by the river Euphrates.

Obadiah 1:15 For the day of the LORD is near upon all the heathen: as thou hast done, it shall be done unto thee: thy reward shall return upon thine own head.

I am pretty sure that Elijah will be one of the two witnesses that are described in Revelation chapter 11. According to Revelation chapter 11 the nations will overrun Jerusalem for 3 1/2 years. Also the two witnesses will prophesy for 3 1/2 years.

Rev 11:2-3 But the court which is without the temple leave out, and measure it not; for it is given unto the Gentiles: and the holy city shall they tread under foot forty and two months. 3 And I will give power unto my two witnesses, and they shall prophesy a thousand two hundred and threescore days, clothed in sackcloth.

It seems that the two witnesses will be killed and resurrected near the end of the tribulation period. If that is the case then they will begin to prophesy during the middle of the tribulation period. That means that Elijah will come during the middle of the seven year Tribulation period.

The next verse happens just after the two witnesses are killed and resurrected.

Rev 11:15 And the seventh angel sounded; and there were great voices in heaven, saying, The kingdoms of this world are become the kingdoms of our Lord, and of his Christ; and he shall reign for ever and ever.

The day of the Lord seems to primarily indicate the day that Jesus returns to fight against the armies that he has gathered together. Just before the day of the Lord, the sun shall be darkened. When Jesus fights against his enemies then the earth will melt with heat.

I agree that the entire seven year Tribulation period is a time of God's wrath. I agree that God will pour out judgments upon the earth during the Tribulation. The Revelation seal judgments seem to fall on the earth in general. Such trials as earthquakes, famines, disease, tidal waves, hail, fire, blood, wild animals, and wars will happen throughout the entire seven year tribulation period. The day of the Lord seems to fall on the rebellious nations and armies that God has purposely gathered together so that he can destroy them in person.

While it is important to note that God will pour out his judgments upon the earth throughout the tribulation period; "The great and dreadful day of the LORD" definitely refers to Jesus Christ's second coming when he will personally judge the nations that have gathered against Israel.

Elijah will come before the second coming of Jesus or what the Bible calls "the day of the LORD". Elijah will continue for 3 ½ years. The Bible does not say that Elijah will come before the Antichrist. The Bible doesn't say that Elijah will come before the seven years long tribulation period begins. The real and original Elijah will come to Jerusalem during the middle of the Tribulation period to turn the hearts of the Jews back towards their God. Then Jesus will return to judge the gentile nations and to restore the nation of Israel.

More from High Time to Awake

Available from Amazon.com, CreateSpace.com, and other retail outlets. Also available on Kindle and other devices.

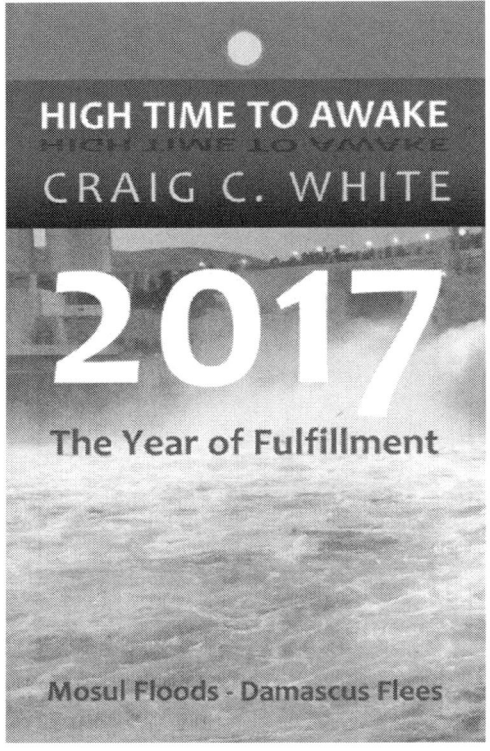

2017 The Year of Fulfillment: The year 2017 will bring several significant Bible prophecies to fruition. This is a serious course of events. A terrible time of trouble for Israel is about to begin. God's judgement is also about to come upon the entire world. It looks like end time Bible prophecy will begin in earnest this year!

hightimetoawake.com

Chapter Thirty

We are about to find out who is correct regarding Daniel chapter 8

By Craig C. White

Iran is objecting to the Turkish offensives in Syria. Well here is something worth considering. Some Bible teachers think that Turkey will attack Iran before the Antichrist rises. Some Bible teachers think that all of Daniel chapter 8 will happen during the end time. I don't think so but we are all about to find out.

Daniel chapter 8 outlines the rise of the Media-Persian Empire as well as the Grecian Empire; so all of Daniel chapter 8 has already been fulfilled. However like many Bible prophesies, history often repeats itself. I don't think that all of Daniel chapter 8 will be repeated but it is obvious that the references to the Grecian governor Antiochus Epiphanies in Daniel chapter 8 are also references to the end time Antichrist. The New Testament tells us that the Antichrist will do many of the same things that Antiochus Epiphanies did long ago. The Antichrist will defile the newly built temple in Jerusalem (Dan 8:12-13, Mat 24:15). The Antichrist will exalt himself above the God of Israel (Dan 8:11, 2Th 2:4). The Antichrist will be empowered by Satan (Dan 8:23-25, 2Th 2:9-10). So we are very certain that at least some of the references to Antiochus Epiphanies in Daniel chapter 8 also apply to the end time Antichrist.

But what about the rest of Daniel chapter 8? Will the Grecian Empire again attack the Persian Empire? Bible prophecy teacher Joel Richardson says yes, sort of. Joel equates the Grecian Empire of long ago to Turkey today. Richardson says that the name *Yavan* or *Javan* that is translated as *Grecia* in Dan 8:21 can refer to Greece and also to Turkey. I want to say that it is pretty clear that Grecia or Yavan refers to Greece in Daniel chapter 8 and also in world history. Nevertheless Yavan is typically located just to the west of

Turkey in the Greek Isles so Yavan isn't too far away from far western Turkey.

Joel Richardson points to the following verse in order to conclude that all of Daniel chapter 8 has end time application. Daniel's vision is being interpreted by the angel Gabriel beginning at Daniel 8:19.

Dan 8:19 And he said, Behold, I will make thee know what shall be in the last end of the indignation: for at the time appointed the end shall be.

Gabriel then quickly identifies the Media-Persian Empire as well as the Grecian Empire but doesn't describe any of their actions. The angel Gabriel does detail the actions of the end time Antichrist through the similar actions of Antiochus Epiphanies. So I would expect that only the details that are explained by Gabriel and that are also reiterated in the New Testament will be repeated during the end time. That means that I don't think that Turkey will attack Iran at this time.

Let me say that I like Joel Richardson a lot. He is one of our very best Bible prophecy teachers. His view on Daniel chapter 8 is respectable.

Joel Richardson says that Turkey will attack Iran and overthrow the Iranian government. That is somewhat feasible since Turkey and Iran are now at odds over Syria. However, that scenario is not reiterated elsewhere in the Bible, especially not in the New Testament. So I don't expect Turkey to attack Iran at this time.

Here is a side note: Joel Richardson concludes that since Greece first had a great king in Alexander the great; but that his empire was broken up and another king rose up (namely Antiochus Epiphanies), that another king will rise out of Turkey to become the Antichrist. I disagree. All of Daniel chapter 8 does not apply to the end time. There is nothing to prevent us from Identifying Turkish President Erdogan as the Antichrist.

If all of Daniel chapter 8 applies to end time events then we should expect Turkey to attack Iran now. If Turkey does not attack Iran now then that should open Joel Richardson's understanding that Turkish President Erdogan is in fact the Antichrist. We don't need to wait for another king to arise out of Turkey. We are about to find out who is correct regarding Daniel chapter 8.

Chapter Thirty One

U.S. Embassy to be moved to Jerusalem in May!

Will the U.S. Embassy become a place of refuge?

By Craig C. White

A temporary U.S. Embassy will be built in the Arnona neighborhood of South Jerusalem. The Trump administration plans to open the new embassy coinciding with Israel's seventy year anniversary of independence on May 14th, 2018. A permanent location is still being sought.

U.S. President Donald Trump intends to move the U.S. Embassy in Israel from Tel Aviv to Jerusalem. This would declare Jerusalem as the rightful capital of Israel. President Trump said that it will take three or four years to build the permanent embassy. Nobody yet knows exactly where the permanent U.S. Embassy will be built but I am certain that the government of Israel will do everything that they can to accommodate the building of the new embassy.

I wonder if the U.S. Embassy will become a place of refuge for the last Jews in Jerusalem.

I know that the Jews living in Judea are instructed to flee into the Judean wilderness when the Antichrist attacks Jerusalem BUT the Jews that are caught inside of Jerusalem are told to wait on Mount Zion for their Messiah to return.

When the Antichrist attacks Jerusalem God instructs the Jews there to return and rest. Anyone who tries to flee Jerusalem will be captured (Isa 30:16). Then the residue of the city will huddle together on Mount Zion (which is the "City of David") in Jerusalem and wait for their redeemer.

Isa 30:15-18 For thus saith the Lord GOD, the Holy One of Israel; In returning and rest shall ye be saved; in quietness and in confidence shall be your strength: and ye would not. 16 But ye said, No; for we will flee upon horses; therefore shall ye flee: and, We will ride upon the

swift; therefore shall they that pursue you be swift. 17 One thousand shall flee at the rebuke of one; at the rebuke of five shall ye flee: till ye be left as a beacon upon the top of a mountain, and as an ensign on an hill. 18 And therefore will the LORD wait, that he may be gracious unto you, and therefore will he be exalted, that he may have mercy upon you: for the LORD is a God of judgment: blessed are all they that wait for him. 19 For the people shall dwell in Zion at Jerusalem: thou shalt weep no more: he will be very gracious unto thee at the voice of thy cry; when he shall hear it, he will answer thee.

Mount Zion is located to the south of the Temple Mount. Mount Zion is also called the city of David. The city of David is the oldest and original site of the city of Jerusalem. Let's see if the permanent U.S. Embassy will be placed in the city of David.

For the U.S. Embassy to become the prophetic place of refuge it would need to be built in the city of David (or Mount Zion). It would also need to be built before the middle of the seven year long Tribulation period. That is when the Antichrist will attack Jerusalem beginning Jerusalem's great tribulation. The Bible says that for any Jews to be saved who have been caught inside of Jerusalem when the Antichrist attacks they must return and wait on Mount Zion. These are those Jews who have not been subjected to death, captivity, hardship, or starvation.

Concerning moving the U.S. Embassy to Jerusalem; Turkish President Erdogan said, "Mr. Trump, Jerusalem is a red line for all Muslims". "We will gather the whole of the Muslim world".

Now do you believe me when I say that Turkish President Erdogan is the Antichrist?

Chapter Thirty Two

Here Al-Qaeda there Al-Qaeda

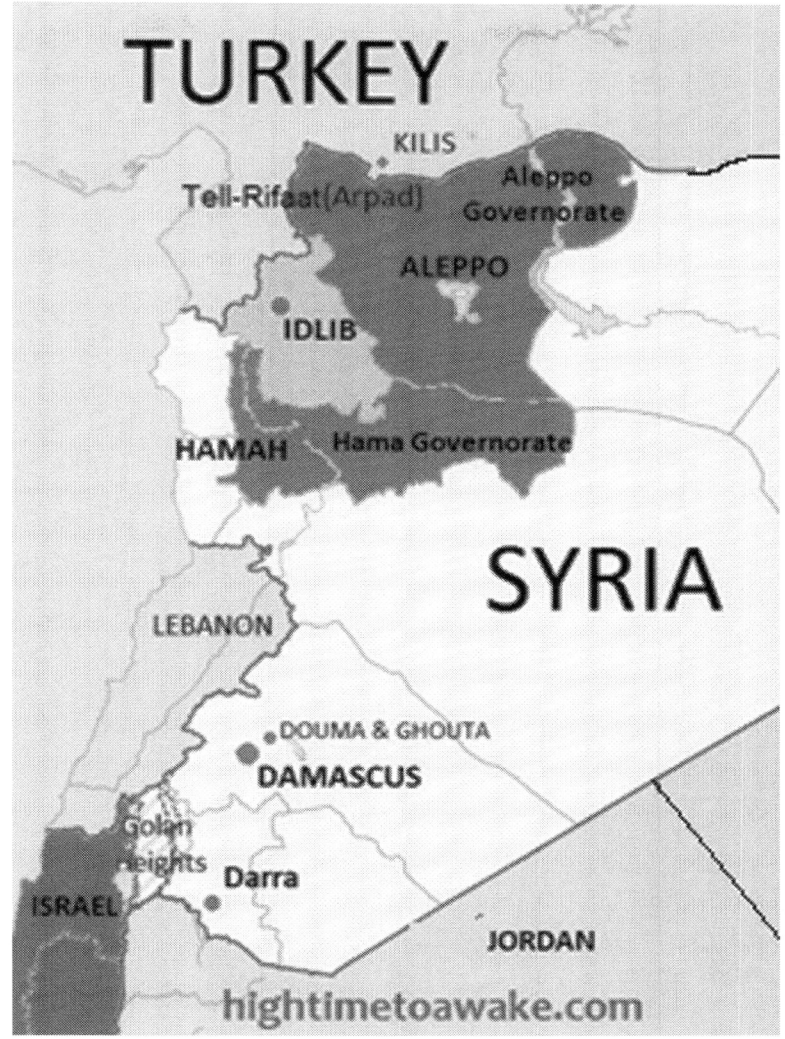

Copyright 2018 Craig C. White

Turkey will redeploy Al-Qaeda against Syria

By Craig C. White

Do you remember when the Syrian Army ousted Al-Qaeda rebels from the northern Damascus neighborhoods of Douma and Ghouta? You might recall that chemical weapons were allegedly used on civilians there. Well those Al-Qaeda rebels were evacuated to the Idlib province in northwestern Syria. Now the Syrian Army is clearing Al-Qaeda rebels out of the Daraa neighborhood located to the south of Damascus. The Syrian regime has allowed safe passage for those Al-Qaeda rebels to Idlib. Idlib was already filled to the brim with Al-Qaeda factions. The Turkish Army is also in Idlib. The Free Syrian Army is yet another Al-Qaeda group that is fighting alongside of the Turkish Army in Idlib. Just so that you know; most of the Al-Qaeda groups in Syria have recently organized under Turkish leadership.

Now that most Al-Qaeda factions have been consolidated in Idlib, people are starting to worry that Turkey will redeploy these rebel groups against the Assad regime and the Syrian Army. This would make the Syrian war it's bloodiest yet. I am here to tell you that Turkey certainly will redeploy these Al-Qaeda rebels.

The Turkish Army is amassed in Idlib near Hamah and also near Tell Rifaat in the Afrin region. The Prophet Jeremiah says that the northwestern Syria cities of Hamah and Tell Rifaat will hear evil reports and then Damascus will be destroyed. Tell Rifaat is called Arpad in Jeremiah 49:23.

Jeremiah 49:23 Concerning Damascus. Hamath is confounded, and Arpad: for they have heard evil tidings: they are fainthearted; there is sorrow on the sea; it cannot be quiet.

All of these Al-Qaeda factions in Idlib are Sunni Muslim. All of these Al-Qaeda factions are fighting against Syrian President Assad. You would think that since they share common beliefs and goals that they would get along but they don't. Now that all of these various Al-Qaeda groups have been crammed together in Idlib, they are fighting each other. This is not an all-out war but they are fighting and killing each other for control over strategic military positions inside of Idlib. That reminds me of a prophecy in Ezekiel chapter 38.

Ezekiel chapter 38 describes Turkey as they lead Iran, Libya, and Sudan into Israel. These are the forces that are fighting in Syria today. Ezekiel 38:21 says that God will cause these invaders to fight against each other when they enter Israel.

Ezekiel 38:21 And I will call for a sword against him throughout all my mountains, saith the Lord GOD: every man's sword shall be against his brother.

The Turkish Army will soon redeploy these disparate Al-Qaeda groups against Hamah and Tell Rifaat. Afterwards Turkey will lead them southward to destroy Damascus. After Turkey destroys Damascus then they will lead the forces that are now fighting in Syria into northern Israel. The Golan Heights are just thirty miles south of Damascus. When they enter Israel God will cause them to fight against each other. But that's not all. Jesus will return to turn them back and also to collect his Church.

More from High Time to Awake

Available from Amazon.com, CreateSpace.com, and other retail outlets. Also available on Kindle and other devices.

Judea Flee! Jerusalem Wait! This book is written and dedicated to the Jews living in Jerusalem and Judea. There is a surprise ambush coming! When you are living your lives in relative peace an army will sweep in and overtake you.

hightimetoawake.com

Chapter Thirty Three

Syria/Russia promise to attack Idlib in September 2018

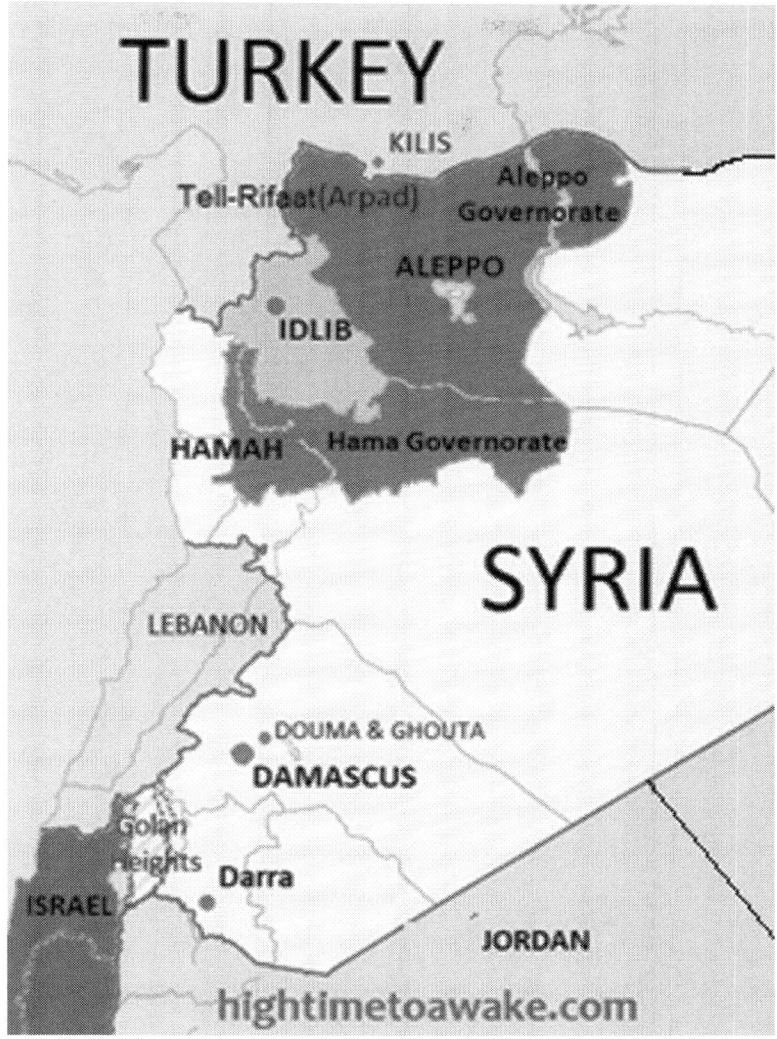

Copyright 2018 Craig C. White

By Craig C. White

After the Syrian Army finishes clearing the Al-Qaeda rebels from the Daraa neighborhood south of Damascus they say that they will begin clearing Idlib in northwestern Syria.

Turkey warned Syria not to attack Idlib. Turkey says that Idlib is a red line.

The Syrian Army controls the Hamah province located to the west and south of Idlib. Over the past few months the Syrian Army in Hamah has intensified their attacks on the Al-Qaeda rebels in Idlib. Russia is promising to provide air strikes in Idlib beginning in September. This will certainly result in a Turkish led attack on Hamah.

The Prophet Jeremiah says that after Hamah and Arpad (or modern day Tell Rifaat) hears evil reports then the residents of Damascus will flee and Damascus will be destroyed.

Jeremiah 49:23 Concerning Damascus. Hamath is confounded, and Arpad: for they have heard evil tidings: they are fainthearted; there is sorrow on the sea; it cannot be quiet.

Jeremiah says that Hamah and Tell Rifaat will hear evil reports and will be terrified. Those evil reports are that the Turkish Army is about to attack. Jeremiah goes on to say that when Hamah and Tell Rifaat hear these reports that the residents of Damascus will flee. We shouldn't have to wait for very long before we hear about Turkey's intentions to attack Hamah.

I've been telling people about this for seven years from the Scriptures. Now it is about to happen. Consider yourself fortunate if you are reading this because the Christian Church is oblivious to the real Bible prophecy that is unfolding in front of their eyes. After Turkey attacks Hamah they will then destroy Damascus. After Turkey destroys Damascus they will then lead the forces that are now fighting in Syria into the Golan Heights of northern Israel. Jesus will return to turn them back and also to collect his Church. So now is the only time that you will ever have to be alert and watching. Jesus told the Church to watch or there will be consequences. It is High Time to Awake!

###

Please review my books on amazon! My Bible prophecy books are on the cutting edge of biblical understanding. Please read one of my books and then write a review on amazon. That way you will help others to know that my books are worth reading. Thank you, Craig C. White

All of my Bible prophecy books are available on amazon in paperback and also in Kindle eBook.

About the Author

Craig C. White

Craig C. White was born in 1958 and born again in 1964. In the 1980's he was an active member of Calvary Church in Santa Ana, California. The expositional Bible teaching of then pastor Dr. David Hocking played a major role in building Craig's biblical literacy. He has been a serious Bible student ever since.

The views contained in my commentaries are solely my own. I do not accept other views just because they are popular. I try to understand what the Bible says. You will find clear and accurate interpretations here that you will scarcely find elsewhere.

www.hightimetoawake.com

More from High Time to Awake

Available from Amazon.com, CreateSpace.com, and other retail outlets. Also available on Kindle and other devices.

Presenting the Antichrist and False Prophet: President **Recep Tayyip Erdogan** is the Antichrist. He is Magog the primary governor of Turkey. He will invade Syria and then invade Israel. The Antichrist will be revealed with blasphemy, false wonders, and a seven year peace agreement concerning Israel. Turkish President Erdogan has recently claimed that he is god, and has also performed false miracles. Erdogan has also fulfilled several other Bible prophecies that identify him as the Antichrist.

There remains a serious threat to Erdogan's power. His name is **Fethullah Gulen**. Fethullah Gulen is an unconventional Muslim cleric who heads an organization all about Islamic indoctrination and world supremacy. He will become the *false prophet*

hightimetoawake.com

13456255R00073

Made in the USA
Middletown, DE
17 November 2018